Re-Forming the Liturgy

Re-Forming the Liturgy

Past, Present, and Future

PAUL GALBREATH

Foreword by Cláudio Carvalhaes

Original Drawings by Tara Taber

CASCADE *Books* · Eugene, Oregon

RE-FORMING THE LITURGY
Past, Present, and Future

Cascade Books
An Imprint of Wipf and Stock Publishers
199 W. 8th Ave., Suite 3
Eugene, OR 97401

www.wipfandstock.com

PAPERBACK ISBN: 978-1-5326-5029-1
HARDCOVER ISBN: 978-1-5326-5030-7
EBOOK ISBN: 978-1-5326-5031-4

Cataloguing-in-Publication data:

Names: Galbreath, Paul, author. | Carvalhaes, Cláudio, foreword. | Taber, Tara, illustrator.

Title: Re-forming the liturgy : past, present, and future / Paul Galbreath ; foreword by Cláudio Carvalhaes ; original drawings by Tara Taber.

Description: Eugene, OR : Cascade Books, 2019 | Includes bibliographical references.

Identifiers: ISBN 978-1-5326-5029-1 (paperback) | ISBN 978-1-5326-5030-7 (hardcover) | ISBN 978-1-5326-5031-4 (ebook)

Subjects: LCSH: Public worship—Reformed Church. | Reformed Church—Liturgy. | Calvin, Jean,—1509-1564. | Reformation. | Worship. | Liturgics.

Classification: BX9422.3 .G35 2019 (paperback) | BX9422.3 .G35 (ebook)

Manufactured in the U.S.A.   04/10/19

I am grateful for the permission to include earlier versions of some of these essays in this collection.

Ch. 1: The Curious Case of the Collect: Between Form and Freedom appeared in *The Collect in the Churches of the Reformation*. London: Hymns Ancient & Modern, 2012.

Ch. 3: The Historical Development of the Season of Easter: Lessons for Liturgical Renewal (with Cláudio Carvalhaes) appeared in Interpretation: A Journal of Bible and Theology, Vol. 64, January, 2011, SAGE Ltd. Publishing.

Ch. 5 and 7: Preaching as Cultivating a Sacramental Imagination (Vol. 25, 2010) and Re-examining our Sacramental Language and Practices (Vol. 31, 2016) appeared in Liturgy, Taylor and Francis.

Ch. 6: Sacramental Models for Daily Life appeared in Theology in Service of the Church. Louisville: Geneva Press, 2008

For Taluli, beloved granddaughter

Contents

Foreword

TO WRITE AN INTRODUCTION to Prof. Paul Galbreath's new book is an honor and a gift. It is not often that we are invited to write about people whom we deeply admire and love. Prof. Galbreath embraced me from the first time we saw each other at Stony Point Center in New York in 2003 at a conference he organized around Worship and the Arts. From that day, he loved me and cared for me deeply. In simple words, I would not be where I am without the wisdom, teachings and companionship of Prof. Galbreath, a man of many gifts, a father, a husband, a grandpa, a pastor, a friend, a man who carries the unbearable lightness of being that Milan Kundera talks about, which is a quality that is not easy to find.

I have witnessed Gabreath's trajectory from the time he worked in the Office of Theology and Worship of the Presbyterian Church (U.S.A.) to his work teaching at Union Presbyterian Seminary in Richmond and now in Charlotte. Galbreath is one of the few people I know who completed two PhDs: one in Biblical Studies from Baylor University and one in Systematic Theology at the University of Heidelberg. Out of his many publications, his first book is my favorite, a very unique work on liturgical theology grounded in the work of the philosopher Ludwig Wittgenstein called *Doxology and Theology: An Investigation of the Apostles' Creed in Light of Ludwig Wittgenstein*. Galbreath has always loved the church and since the beginning of his seminary teaching at Union, he has always made clear he wanted to publish for the church. His trilogy composed of *Leading from the Table, Leading through the Water,* and *Leading into the World* is a work of love to the church. Not a work of love in a Kierkegardian sense, marked by an *anguished conscience* and the typical passive-aggressiveness of Luther and many of his disciples but rather, as an existentialist like Camus, one who loves life both quietly but in almost desperate ways.

This new book is yet another expression of love to the Reformed faith, with articles on Reformed worship he has written throughout his academic career. With a variety of focused points, Galbreath divides his book into a timely frame: past, present, and future. These timely frames can be elusive if the reader tries to hold the articles locked in these categories. On the contrary, these times blur into each other, accessing a full sense of time all together in each article. For instance, the article on Eucharist placed in the past is a fundamental source for our present theology. The articles on the sacramentality of our lives and the possibility of new practices of our faith now shapes us into the future. And all of the ecological work framed in the future begs us to start doing it in the present. The *ora et labora* of Galbreath's book demands us to pray and work together at the same time, all of the time. In other words, the people who do its liturgical work now, pray in a way grounded in the past, aware of the present, and deeply shaped by the future.

At the crux of Galbreath's work lies his Reformed faith and his deep love for the church universal by way of loving his own particular commitment to the Presbyterian Church (U.S.A.). The "Church reformed, always being reformed" is at the heart of these articles as he tries to shake us up into necessary, permanent, and relevant forms in order to "be reformed" today. To be reformed is his understanding of the liturgy as *ora et labora*.

This means that while fundamentally Reformed, Galbreath is free in his living of religious liturgical orders and interfaith practices, guided as he is by the gracious moving of the Holy Spirit. For it is the work of the Holy Spirit that makes him free and at the same time firmly oriented by the confessions of the church and necessarily rooted in Scriptures. From this solid framework, he takes the challenges of our day, perplexed by our times but confident that what we have received by the cloud of witnesses is enough to guide us now and in the future. That is why Galbreath cannot understand why some pastors today fail to find ways to live out the vibrant gospel of Jesus Christ fully in our society. For him, Calvin's reinvention of the community in the sixteenth century is at the heart of our being reformed today and a great example of how leaders of our communities can move within our time, reinventing ourselves in the faith given to us by God that demands us to continue to be reformed. What might trouble some people in Galbreath's work is that while some scholars freeze the Reformation in a cluster of tenets to be repeated *ad nauseam*, Galbreath understands the Reformation as a more vivid movement, alive and pulsing with an energy that carries us with a faith that can speak fully to our time and a grace that can sustain us in this work.

In this path, the church's necessary reinvention cannot depend on the *Book of Common Worship* alone to fulfill its mission. While this liturgical resource is fundamental, it is definitely not enough. This is demonstrated in his own participation in the newly revised *Book of Common Worship* of the PCUSA. However, while he contributed to the book and uses it, he also advocates other liturgical models that can change and reflect the conditions and possibilities where each community is located. For him, faithfulness to the Reformed tradition does not mean faithfulness to a liturgical book alone. While placing the book in every pew might serve as a guide, it won't do what the church needs to do by embodying our prayers in the world around us. His mind and his faith are much bigger than that, and to be reformed demands of us way more than allegiance to a single fixed form.

Another point that marks Galbreath's work is that he is fully invested in the whole work of liturgical renewal. In fact, his entire corpus is nothing more than an attempt to develop the possibilities of the liturgical renewal in new directions. His theology is grounded in it, he is shaped by it, and he developed it through his early work in sacramental ethics while in the worship office of the Presbyterian Church. This approach to liturgical renewal has to do with the amplification of the liturgical life of the church in the world. For that reason, he has no time or interest in being "crypto-catholic," nor in trying to hold on to something that calls itself liturgically faithful to a tradition and hides under that form. No, Galbreath is much freer than that. His primary allegiance is to the world of God where people live and suffer rather than to the smallness and arrogance of specificities of certain liturgical forms of local traditions turned universal by its adherents.

True to the liturgical movement, he wants liturgy to go to the streets, faith seeking understanding through the issues of our day, now especially in and through the *ecos/oikos* of God, suffering due to the ravishes of climate change. Thus, the liturgical movement for him must be faithful to the relation between *ora et labora in* the world, wrestling with tradition as people wrestle with their Reformed identity in this burning world.

That is why he rejects certain approaches to liturgical renewal in our days. As an example, being a biblical scholar, he is concerned with the ways that the ecumenical liturgical calendar deals with Scripture and thus distances himself on this issue from many Catholics, Anglicans, or Lutherans when the use of the liturgical year and feast days ends up filtering the lectionary readings through particular gospel texts. Thus, the use of the liturgical calendar in the liturgical movement runs opposite to the ways Calvin used Scripture when it eradicates a primary commitment to the sufficiency of both Old and New Testament texts as testimonies to our encounters with the divine. Similarly, Galbreath remains firmly grounded to a Reformed identity that affirms the primacy of communal life, the living of a corporate kind of piety, and particular ways of celebrating the sacraments. For example, in the Reformed perspective, baptism fundamentally belongs to the community and is not a private transaction between clergy and individuals, but a lifelong journey of discipleship. This path is not an easy one. Galbreath walks a thin rope trying to balance the Reformed faith with the challenges of our world; his faithfulness to the liturgical renewal with the necessity of new liturgical creation. The juxtaposition of this set of sometimes clashing issues serves only and fundamentally to make the church of Jesus Christ be what it must be: God's living witness in the world, bringing freedom to the captive and lifting up the weary. In order to do that, the church moves through a process where a living faithfulness to the Reformed tradition, handed down in historical process, makes the church be always reformed, attentive, and fully present before God in our time.

His reformed commitment to the church is accompanied by his personal faith in Christ. The author of this book doesn't shy away from having been brought up as a Baptist who, strangely enough, affirms not only his deep commitment to the liturgical renewal but to the whole transformation of the world. His personal Christian faith found in the Reformed pattern is the only way to be lived: life that is shared together in community. Perhaps because of his religious upbringing, Galbreath is allergic to a pious individual spirituality that does not assert itself collectively. Perhaps this is why he can see the ins and outs of the individualistic patterns of the liturgical movement in ways that many cannot. There is no Christian faith if not lived together, and no liturgical renewal if not in a more expansive social and political frame, engaging the historical times in contextual locations where churches can thus transform the world.

That is why form and freedom is at the forefront of his liturgical work. Form and freedom time and again. Since he is also existentially wounded, Galbreath carries Camus's troubled heart, Munch's scream, Van Gogh's yellows, and the haunting unfinished forms of Giacometti. Freedom and sorrow, love, joy, and abundance carry his heart. He has always lived Ecclesiastes fully! His own sense of mortality frees him from the strictures of those who hold on to fixed forms of liturgy as a way of faithfulness often hiding behind immense forms of fear. He is beyond that. Wisely, he can worship God in a fixed liturgy, but he can also glorify God in various unstructured forms of worship.

Galbreath's work has much to give us. The last section of this book I believe is the most critical one for our time. For me, there is nothing that makes sense today if not done in light of the pressing concerns and the needs of the earth. Without an ecological view, there is no reason for us to do anything. The struggle for the Earth is our sum zero. What is the point of liturgical renewal or any tradition if we are destroying the creation, the *oikos* of God? Galbreath is leading the way by presenting paths for us to take. I pray we can learn from him and awaken to do this work together.

Cláudio Carvalhaes
August 2018
Union Theological Seminary in NYC

Preface

THIS BRIEF COLLECTION OF essays shows the evolution of the work that I have been doing in liturgical theology over the past fifteen years. The arrangement of the chapters is not in chronological order, but follows a three-step pattern that traces the work of liturgical renewal. The movement in these essays is ultimately ongoing and circular in nature and recognizes any liturgical event or text as provisional in nature, i.e., for the proclamation of the gospel in a particular time and place and for those who have gathered in that unique space. For the purpose of this book, I have divided the essays into three groups. The first group looks at the critical, analytical work that is required in order to discover the ways in which our liturgical texts can be re-formed. In this section, I am particularly interested in showing how liturgical renewal in the Reformed tradition has gone about the work of renewal.

The second part of this book looks at the material with which we have to work, namely Word and Sacrament, as the building blocks in the creation of new liturgical forms to serve the church. Here the reader will see evidence of ways in which tradition plays a key role in the creation of new liturgical resources for the church: Scripture read and proclaimed and the celebration of the sacraments of baptism and communion provide central elements around which the church hears and responds to the good news of the gospel.

The third and final section of this monograph focuses on the ways in which liturgies can constructively engage one of the most critical ethical issues of our time: climate change and the ecological crisis that we have created and to which we must respond. These essays push us towards creative efforts in liturgical renewal that both support and move us into action.

What began initially as a focus on sacramental ethics as a way of insisting on more clearly articulated and embodied connections between worship and daily life has moved towards a focus on eco-liturgical themes as one way of showing the need for vigilant and persistent work that holds our worship texts and communities accountable. I have been helped along the way by many people who have influenced, challenged, and shaped the way that I approach this work. I am particularly grateful to my colleague and friend, Cláudio Carvalhaes, whose own work on liturgical renewal continues to chart important new directions in liturgical theology. I am also appreciative of those who have responded to these ideas in places where I have presented them: members of the Ecology and Worship seminar at the North American Academy of Liturgy as well as participants in conferences of the Journey for Baptismal Living, the Institute of Sacred Music's gathering on Liturgy and Cosmology, and Presbyterians for Earth Care. Some of these essays originally appeared in journals and books, so I am thankful for the permission to revise and include them in this work. My thanks goes out to Anna Cwikla who provided initial editorial assistance on this project. This book is dedicated to our granddaughter Taluli, who is the light of our lives, in the hope and prayer that people of faith will work for a better world.

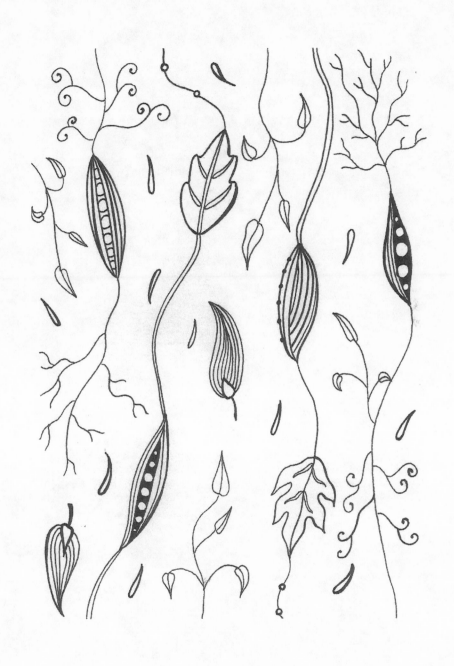

PART ONE

Liturgical Lessons from the Past

WE LIVE IN AN era of turmoil and change on nearly every front. In the midst of these significant transitions, congregations are searching for ways to embody the gospel that address the deep concerns in their own lives and in their communities. Of course, these challenges are not entirely new to Christian communities, which have frequently struggled to discover appropriate and faithful ways to live out the gospel in their own unique times and conditions. The history of the Reformed tradition shows an ongoing tension between the desire to embody a renewed understanding of the church in light of the guiding witness of communities that are portrayed in Scripture. In fact, the watchword of Reformed Christians captures this sense of the constant back and forth movement between biblical images and resources and their embodiment in particular communities of faith. As noted in the constitution of the Presbyterian Church (U.S.A.), "*Ecclesia reformata, semper reformanda verbum Dei*, that is, 'The Church reformed, always to be reformed according to the Word of God,' in the power of the Spirit."[1] At stake in this declaration is a lively balancing act of renewing the life of the church in light of the witness of Scripture and in accordance with the movement of the Spirit.

At times, Reformed communities have erred in the manners in which they have interpreted this adage. For some, the role of Scripture in defining the identity of the community has resulted in forms of biblical literalism that have demanded scriptural proof texts for any part of worship. A quick

1. Presbyterian Church (U.S.A.), *Constitution of the Presbyterian Church (U.S.A.)*, F-2.02.

1

glance at *The Book of Common Worship* still shows how each movement in worship is connected with specific biblical citations. In this instance, the dynamic nature of diverse biblical communities has been overlooked as well as the need for communities to articulate and embody the gospel in their own particular contexts. For others, the Spirit's involvement in the messy business of liturgical inculturation has provided a precedence for adopting that which is new, sometimes at the expense of any guidance from Scripture. The challenge remains to navigate these stormy waters by carefully and deliberately steering a course that takes its cues from the diverse witness of Scripture while exploring ways to faithfully embody the call of the gospel in our lives in our own circumstances. Here, the work of liturgical history can provide insights in ways that diverse communities of faith have addressed similar challenges in their own situations.

In the following three essays, we will explore themes and clues that can guide communities of faith to rediscover ways that can shape our gatherings and lives. In the first essay, we examine the role of a particular form of prayer, the collect, in order to identify the ways in which Reformed Christians have adapted this way of praying to express our own particular theological identity. At stake in this study is the chance to discover authentic ways of praying that articulate deep theological convictions that are part of our identity as followers of Jesus Christ. The second essay explores John Calvin's theological interpretation of the role of the Law in order to ascertain the ways in which this can shape our own practices of Christian formation. Calvin's broad perspective on the theological *telos* of the Law underscores the ways that deeply connect our baptismal and vocational identity and offer us suggestions of how to live out a vision of communal life. The final essay in this section surveys the historical development of the season of Easter in order to imagine how this liturgical season can be embodied in diverse communities of faith. Together these three essays demonstrate the ways in which liturgical and theological lessons from the past can guide us in identifying patterns for Christian living that draw on the wisdom of those who have gone before us while opening up possibilities for faithful responses that Christians can embody in our lives of faith today.

1

The Curious Case of the Collect

Between Form and Freedom

A DELIBERATE TENSION BETWEEN form and freedom lies at the center of liturgical practice in the Reformed tradition.[1] Since the dramatic reform of worship practices in Strasbourg and Geneva during the sixteenth century, Reformed ecclesial bodies have drawn on the historic shape and pattern of liturgical forms while at the same time creating space for these forms to be articulated and embodied in distinctive ways. The history of the collect in the Reformed tradition includes a narrative of use, neglect, and transformation that enlightens not only the Reformed approach to this

---

1. This tension is presented as a basic principle of worship in the Directory for Worship that is a part of the constitution of the Presbyterian Church (U.S.A.). Note the wording in *The Constitution of the Presbyterian Church (U.S.A.)*, Part II, Book of Order, Directory for Worship: "The Church has always experienced a tension between form and freedom in worship. In the history of the church, some have offered established forms for ordering worship in accordance with God's Word. Others, in the effort to be faithful to the Word, have resisted imposing any fixed forms upon the worshipping community. The Presbyterian Church (U.S.A.) acknowledges that all forms of worship are provisional and subject to reformation. In ordering worship the church is to seek openness to the creativity of the Holy Spirit, who guides the church toward worship which is orderly yet spontaneous, consistent with God's Word and open to the newness of God's future" (W-3.1002).

particular prayer, but also points to the broader liturgical practices within the Reformed tradition.

Before beginning this historical survey, the reader should be aware of two disclaimers. First, it is, of course, impossible to provide a full picture of the approach to any particular liturgical practice in a tradition as broad and diverse as Reformed congregations. As a result, this chapter looks briefly at historical snapshots of the use and adaptation of the collect at particular times and places in Reformed churches. Secondly, by its nature, the Reformed tradition is a highly varied and sometimes eclectic collection of congregations whose shared liturgical identity is grounded in particular readings and interpretations of Scripture and who exercise broad parameters for liturgical interpretation and adaptation to take place. This survey will pay attention to the use and adaptation of the collect particularly in Reformed bodies in the United States, with special attention to the practices of the Presbyterian Church (U.S.A.).[2] The purpose of this focus is not to overlook the significance of Reformed bodies around the world, but to illustrate the adaptive liturgical principles used in the collects in Reformed history.

THE HISTORICAL ROOTS OF THE COLLECT

In his essay entitled, "The Collect in Context," Patrick Regan describes the teleological aim of the collect as providing a "culminating point of all that comes before the service of the word."[3] Regan describes the place of the collect in the oldest extant account of a papal Mass, the *Ordo Romanus Primus*, which comes from eighth-century Rome. Here, the collect clearly fulfills the role of bringing the opening movement of the Mass to completion. The entrance rite includes the procession of the liturgical leaders of the assembly, a sung psalm, *Gloria Patri*, *Kyrie Eleison*, and *Gloria in Excelsis Deo*. Then, the presider offers the collect as prayer that closes this opening act of the liturgy.

Similarly, James White describes the development of the liturgy at an even earlier time of liturgical transition. White notes that the rapid expansion of Christianity in the fourth-century Roman Empire brought change

2. In particular, the essay concludes with an examination of the place of the collect in the Presbyterian Church (U.S.A.) and in the denominations that led up to the historic reunion of Presbyterian churches in the North and South.

3. Regan, "Collect in Context," 96.

to liturgical practice as a matter of necessity. The move to larger spaces for Christian assembly came with a need to adapt practices for the gathering of worshipers. Thus, White describes the expansion of the opening of the rite as providing traveling music to allow the procession of clergy to move to the front of the assembly and take their places in the liturgical assembly. Once gathered in this manner, the collect brings this opening act to a conclusion.[4]

Regan helpfully describes the collect's summative nature in both the High Mass and the Low Mass as that which brings the entrance rite to full fruition. The collect offers the first occasion for the presider's voice to be heard by the assembly and the completion of the opening movement in the service leads to a change in the assembly's posture, who are seated following the "Amen."[5] This descriptive analysis leads Regan to conclude that "the collect shines forth in all its pristine splendor as both the culmination and conclusion of the entrance procession."[6]

REFORMATION TRANSFORMATIONS

I have underscored this analysis of the role and place of the collect in its historical development in order to contrast it with the liturgical development of the sixteenth century Protestant Reformation. In Germany, Martin Luther's approach to liturgical reform has been characterized as conservative and evangelical.[7] Luther describes the place of the collect at the end of the opening rite in his work *Formula missae and Deutsche Messe:*

> In the third place, the *Oratio* (prayer), or Collect which follows, if it is pious (and those appointed for the Lord's Days usually are), should be preserved in its accustomed use; but there should be but one.[8]

---

4. White, *Introduction to Christian Worship,* 156. White's own description of the role of the collect as that which "concludes the introductory rite" and "introduces the lessons for the day" offers a distinct parallel to the developments of the collect in the Reformed tradition.

5. Regan, "Collect in Context," 98.

6. Regan, "Collect in Context," 99.

7. See Thompson, *Liturgies of the Western Church,* 100.

8. Luther in Thompson, *Liturgies of the Western Church,* 109.

Thus, for Luther, the primary change was to limit the collect to one prayer instead of multiple prayers, a practice that had developed at this point in the service.[9]

By contrast, the liturgical reformation of the congregations where John Calvin served in Strasbourg and Geneva involved clearer distinctions from earlier practice and sometimes the transformation of received practices, as they are grounded in a distinctive theological framework. The precursor to these changes is generally identified as the revisions to the Mass in Strasbourg made by Diebold Schwarz. On February 16, 1524, Schwarz celebrated Mass in German in St. John's Chapel in the cathedral in Strasbourg. Significant changes included the congregation's participation in the *Confiteor* (confession) which had previously been said by the priest alone.[10] Schwarz's service became the model for the service outlined by the German Protestant reformer Martin Bucer for use in Strasbourg and other Reformed congregations. The order of the opening rite included confession of sin, scriptural words of pardon, absolution, a psalm or hymn, *Kyrie eleison*, *Gloria in excelsis*, a collect for illumination, a metrical psalm, gospel reading, and a sermon.[11] This outline provided a liturgical pattern and theological approach for Calvin's work in Strasbourg and in Geneva.

Reformed worship is grounded in a distinctive reading of Scripture. Thus, following Bucer's lead, Calvin's liturgy begins with a biblical citation: "Our help is the name of the Lord, who made heaven and earth. Amen."[12] This use of Scripture serves as a biblical warrant for the assembly's gathering and leads to a prayer of confession and absolution of pardon to all who repent of their sin. In Strasbourg, these actions were followed by the congregational singing of the Ten Commandments, a way of allowing a biblical text to inform the practices of the covenant community's shared way of life. In Geneva, the prayer of confession was followed by the singing of a psalm by the congregation.[13] In both cases, the congregation's song

9. Regan notes that there could be up to seven prayers offered during medieval times. Regan, "Collect in Context," 98.

10. Barkley, *Worship of the Reformed Church*, 14.

11. Barkley, *Worship of the Reformed Church*, 14–15. One can argue that the singing of two psalms allows the collect for illumination to continue to function as an act of culmination of the opening rite as much as an opening to the reading of the Word. This prayer provides a kind of transitional bridge in the service. As we will see, Calvin's alterations to the order in Geneva cause a more dramatic shift to this prayer.

12. Psalm 124:8 (New Revised Standard Version).

13. The omission of the absolution in the Genevan liturgy is the result of the

serves as the culminating act of the gathering of the assembly for worship. A "collect for illumination" follows this opening rite.[14] Thus, while Calvin maintained the place of the collect in the liturgy, he dramatically altered its function. The prayer no longer primarily served to sum up that which preceded it. Instead, the prayer pointed to that which is to follow, namely the reading of Scripture and the sermon. It is also important to note that in the Genevan liturgy, Calvin described the purpose of this prayer and notes that "the form is left to the discretion of the Minister."[15]

Six primary features of this adaptive liturgical practice come to the forefront. First, Calvin's foundational requirement of the role of the collect for illumination is that the prayer is distinctively pneumatological. The main purpose of the prayer is to request the Spirit's presence to bring insight to the assembly as Scripture is read in order that the Church may hear, understand, and receive the Word read and proclaimed. This distinctive theological approach to Scripture stands over and against those who argued for the perspicuity or clearness of Scripture. Calvin's own commitment to careful exegetical work (a hallmark shared by many others in both Roman Catholic and Protestant communities of the time) remained subservient to the fundamental theological conviction that it is the Holy Spirit that brings to life the interpretation of Scripture. Thus, this particular and distinctive approach to the collect is based firmly on a theological understanding of the role of the Holy Spirit. While there are other aspects and approaches in the development of the collect in the history of Reformed congregations, this particular insight remains fundamental and basic to Reformed churches. This approach to this prayer stands in marked contrast to the classic Roman approach to the collect which Gerard Moore notes typically has an "implicit, rather than explicit pneumatology."[16] Moore's analysis of the Roman collects underscores the central christological framework of the collect in the Roman tradition, which is distinctive in relation to the pneumatological direction of the Reformed approach to the collect.

---

congregation's objection to this practice. "In Strasbourg Calvin supplied an Absolution no less forthright than that of Bucer; but when he returned to Geneva, the people objected to this 'novelty,' illustrating their hostility by jumping up before the end of Confession to forestall an Absolution. Thus he yielded to their scruples." Thompson, *Liturgies of the Western Church*, 191.

14. These orders of worship and an example of this collect may be found in Thompson, *Liturgies of the Western Church*, 197–99.

15. Calvin in Thompson, *Liturgies of the Western Church*, 199.

16. Moore, "Vocabulary of the Collects," 189.

Secondly, Calvin's approach to the collect has a particular aim in mind: illumination. Calvin's theological approach to Scripture became reinforced in this liturgical practice. The prayer seeks guidance from the Spirit in order that the church may understand the reading of Scripture. In contrast to the distinctive doxological aim of the Roman collects, Calvin's approach takes on a particular exhortatory characteristic. The minister beseeches God for grace and guidance from the Holy Spirit in order that God's Word may be faithfully read and heard by the gathering. The ultimate goal for Calvin is the edification of the church.[17] Thus, a particular ecclesiological understanding is implicit in this practice of prayer. For Calvin, the church as the covenant community of the faithful seeks guidance from Scripture through the presence of the Holy Spirit in order to cultivate lives marked by humility and obedience.

Thirdly, for Calvin the collect clearly points towards the basic role of Scripture as foundational for the gathering of the assembly. The collect is an act of preparation in order for the congregation to hear and understand Scripture as it is read and proclaimed. Hence, there is a distinctly biblical framework for this prayer. Moore notes that Roman collects may often employ biblical vocabulary in both implicit and explicit ways throughout the prayers, but that at least some liturgical scholars have argued that the Roman collect is "non-biblical in nature."[18] By contrast, the biblical nature of Reformed collects takes a different turn. Calvin's collect for illumination is a preparatory act for the hearing of particular biblical texts on a particular day by a particular congregation. Thus, the biblical nature of this approach is grounded in a high reverence for Scripture as foundational to the life of the assembly alongside the possibility that the language of the prayer may be shaped and influenced by particular texts read on this occasion.

Fourthly, Calvin's approach to the collect is based on the practice of this prayer being offered by the minister. In place of an established text, the minister is given license to offer a prayer for illumination that is guided by its primary goals. Calvin did provide examples of this prayer, such as this one:

> Almighty and gracious Father, since our whole salvation stand-
> eth in our knowledge of thy Holy Word, strengthen us now by

17. This language of beseeching and edification comes from Calvin's liturgy in Thompson, *Liturgies of the Western Church*, 198–99.

18. Moore's brief outline of the debate about the biblical nature of collects is insightful on this point, Moore, "Vocabulary of the Collects," 176–77, see footnote 5 in particular.

thy Holy Spirit that our hearts may be set free from all worldly thoughts and attachments of the flesh, so that we may hear and receive that same Word, and recognizing thy gracious will for us, may love and serve thee with earnest delight, praising and glorifying thee in Jesus Christ our Lord. Amen.[19]

It is not clear whether Calvin's practice (and those who followed him) was to rely on a written (prepared) collect for illumination or to offer an extemporaneous prayer guided by the primary purpose for this prayer. In either case, it is important to note that this new approach to prayer usurped the place of a shared, historical text.

Fifthly, there is a surprising quality to this prayer that is focused in its style. Compared to other prayers from Calvin's liturgy, this prayer is generally terse in its brevity and focused in its aim. Whereas in places of great liturgical innovation (e.g., communion prayers), Calvin's approach was to include explanatory material to differentiate the current form from previous ones, the collects avoided these tendencies. Perhaps certain patterns from the historic, textual approach to collects which Calvin certainly had experienced in French Roman Catholic churches continued to underlie the construction of the collect for illumination and guide the language to remain lean and focused.

Finally, there is an implicit pedagogy in Calvin's approach to the collect. The desire to nurture piety in the home and in daily life is a hallmark of Calvin's work in the church in Geneva and continues to be a primary constitutive practice of Reformed Christians. Thus, the transformation of the collect with its link to both reading and interpreting Scripture in light of the Spirit's presence in our lives offers a practice that can be readily transported from the Sunday assembly to private household devotions. Calvin's approach to the collect models a distinctive method of prayer that finds its roots in the service for the Lord's Day that encourages participants to use these forms in their daily lives.

19. Calvin adapted this prayer from Bucer, in Thompson, *Liturgies of the Western Church*, 209. It is worth noting the transition in posture in this practice as outlined in the Strasbourg liturgy. The congregation begins the service kneeling and stands for the singing of the law. The first table of the law is followed by a prayer to receive the law and then the congregation stands to sing the second table of the law. Afterwards, the congregation kneels for the prayer for illumination according to the rubrics from *The Calvin Strasbourg Service*. The significance of these movements again points to the transformed role of the collect in the Reformed liturgy in contrast to the Roman use of the collect and the distinctive role of posture that is associated with the collect.

A HERITAGE IN TRANSITION

We have seen how Calvin's distinctive theological approach to the collect brought about a dramatic transformation. While keeping the prayer in the same location of the Sunday assembly, it took on distinctly new features primarily focused on the decision to point the assembly forward to the reading of Scripture rather than the collect's previous primary role of serving to sum up the opening rite. This approach to the collect was furthered by John Knox, who helped bring Calvin's theology and the Reformation practices to the Church of Scotland.

Calvin's liturgy from Strasbourg was translated into German and provided a basis for Knox's work in compiling the *Forme of Prayer* for the Church of Scotland in 1556. Following Calvin, Knox's liturgy noted that after the singing of a psalm by the congregation the minister "prayeth for th' assistance of God's Holy Spirite, as the same move his harte, and so procedeth to the Sermon."[20] Thus, this practice established by Calvin in Geneva became normative for the Church of Scotland. Whereas the Church of England translated ancient Latin prayers for use in the liturgy and crafted new prayers in light of these patterns, the Church of Scotland generally adopted the practice established by Bucer and Calvin in Strasbourg and Geneva. However, a contrasting vision for the role of the collect developed alongside this practice in the Church of Scotland. In 1595, a Scottish Metrical Psalter was published which included a set of prayers in the Scottish dialect for each psalm. This collection of prayers was a translation of the French prayers written by Clement Marot and Theodore de Beze in 1567. The prayers had previously appeared in the French Psalter published in 1561 and are characterized by their reliance on "pre-Reformation liturgies" and have been described as *"nouvellement adjoustées* rather than in the strict sense new."[21] These prayers build on the classic Roman form of the collect which at the time was uncommon in Scottish use. This form is summarized by five distinct parts of the prayer:

1. The invocation

2. The recital of some doctrine or fact of the Faith which is made the basis of the petition

3. The petition itself

20. Knox, *Liturgy of John Knox*, 99.
21. Bannerman's analysis of the prayers in *Scottish Collects*, 6.

4. The aspiration expressive of what the consequence of the petition is expected to be

5. And the pleading of the Name of our Lord as the ground of confidence that the prayer will be accepted.[22]

This Scottish edition of the Psalter prayers followed the earlier form of the Roman collect while expressing the prayer in a distinctly Scottish style. Even here, though, the collection shows a significant shift in the final ten prayers, which "abandoned the collect form" and no longer rely on the earlier French prayers.[23]

The importance of this for our study shows that while the function of the collect in the Lord's Day service radically shifted in light of Calvin's practice in Geneva, an alternative vision of the historic understanding of the collect remained. To cite but one example from this important collection, note the prayer to be read after the reading of Psalm 23:

> Eternal and Everlasting Father, Fountain of all felicity; we render Thee praises and thanks for that Thou hast made known to us our Shepherd and Defender Who shall deliver us from the power of our adversaries. Grant unto us, that we, casting away all fear and terror of death, may embrace and confess Thy truth, which it hath pleased Thee to reveal to us by Thy Son, our Lord and sovereign Master, Christ Jesus.[24]

While the transformation of the Roman collect into a Prayer for Illumination reoriented the practice and understanding of this particular prayer in the Reformed tradition, the older approach to the collect was maintained. It is important to note that these compilations of collects (both the original French prayers and their largely derivative Scottish prayers) were woven into the fabric of the Psalter, a place of distinct importance in Reformed worship. Since the opening rite in the liturgies of Calvin and Knox concluded with the singing of a psalm by the congregation, the development of a set of collects attached to the Psalter provided a form of collective memory of prayers that serve to sum up the movement at a particular place in the service. While Sunday practice in Reformed congregations caused the collect for illumination to point in a different direction, the use of collects

22. These five parts are listed in Bannerman, *Scottish Collects*, 6.

23. Bannerman, *Scottish Collects*, 7.

24. Bannerman, *Scottish Collects*, 16. Some of these prayers have been included in the psalm prayers that are provided in *The Book of Common Worship*.

in daily prayer was preserved in this important collection. As early as the fifth century, Harold Daniels notes that "psalm prayers were replaced by the *Gloria Patri* (q.v.) to defend against Arianism. The restoration of the psalm prayer, following the Second Vatican Council, replaces singing or saying the *Gloria Patri* at the conclusion of a psalm."[25] Ironically, then, one can note that the gift of the collect that was part of the Roman Mass was preserved in an approach to the Psalter in the practices of Daily Prayer in the Reformed tradition until it was recovered by the Roman Catholic Church in the reforms of Vatican II.

THE SHIFT TOWARDS FREEDOM

While forms or at least orders for the liturgy provided a collective pattern for Reformed churches, ongoing disputes between the Church of England and the Church of Scotland created a rift that led to a reexamination of the role of worship books. This issue came to a head in the meeting of the Assembly of Divines at Westminster through the adoption of *The Directory for the Publick Worship of God*, which was approved for use in the Church of Scotland in 1645. In the preface to the *Directory*, the assembly noted the important contributions of prayers and forms that have been provided for the use of the church, but after prayer and study of Scripture called the church to the work of further Reformation:

> To lay aside the former Liturgy, with the many Rites and Ceremonies formerly used in the Worship of God; and have agreed upon this following Directory for all the Parts of publick Worship, at ordinary and extraordinary Times.[26]

The Directory included a brief section on prayer before the sermon. Noteworthy is that after the reading of Scripture and the singing of the psalms "all the prayers for the Lord's Day are drawn up into one body without any dividing of them."[27] In this dramatic move, the distinctive theological and liturgical patterns of the opening liturgical rite of the early Reformed churches is obliterated. In place of distinct forms of prayer in specific texts, a general and extended prayer is offered that is marked largely by confessional and penitential language. *The Directory* offered a suggested shape to

25. Daniels, *To God Alone Be Glory*, 165.
26. *Directory for the Publick Worship*, 9.
27. Leishman, *Westminster Directory*, 89.

this lengthy prayer (the minister is "to call upon the name of the Lord to this Effect") that ultimately concluded with a petition for the preacher and the congregation. This implied request for illumination is transferred from the reading and hearing of Scripture to the proclamation of the Word. The more distinctive act of Calvin's Collect for Illumination became a solitary act of the minister who is encouraged in his work to seek through prayer the illumination of the Spirit as he studies Scripture "in his private Preparations, before he deliver in Publick what he hath provided."[28] This dramatic change prompted one commentator to conclude:

> When one today looks back over this long prayer with its many sub-headings and painfully accurate exposition of every possible occasion, it is no wonder that the verbal portions of the Directory were almost wholly disregarded, and its very prolixity was no doubt the chief reason for its non-use.[29]

In many liturgical matters the *Directory for Worship* remained silent and as a result, its influence on Scottish practice is open to debate.[30] However, the *Westminster Directory* remained normative for the Scottish Church and was adopted by the first General Assembly of the Presbyterian Church in the United States in 1788.

RESTORING ORDER

Liturgical renewal came to the Church of Scotland from one of its original sources. In 1840, the republishing of Knox's liturgy, *The Book of Common Order*, began a prolonged period of reexamination and recovery. In Scotland, the publication of Knox's liturgy restored the role of the Prayer for Illumination. During this same period, the appearance of the *Liturgy and other Divine Offices of the Church* in the Catholic Apostolic Church created a flurry of interest in liturgical reform. By contrast, this liturgy placed the collect before the reading of Scripture.[31]

28. *Directory for the Publick Worship*, 17.

29. Hurlburt, *Liturgy of the Church*, 80. Story comments on the worship practice of the Scottish church at this time that, "The prayers were reduced in number to two at the most, and were drearily long and uninteresting." In Barkley, *Worship of the Reformed Church*, 30–31.

30. On this point in particular, see Barkley, *Worship of the Reformed Church*, 31.

31. The placement of the collect in the Euchologion suggests that the collect functions as a preface to the reading of Scripture rather than in its summative role in the Roman Mass.

In the United States, the Mercersburg movement in the German Reformed Church was led by Phillip Schaff and John Nevin, who published a *Book of Worship* in 1858 that was revised and adopted in 1866. Alongside these efforts of liturgical renewal, the Church Service Society played a decisive role in providing new liturgical resources for the Church of Scotland. These movements sought in various ways to restore liturgical forms to the worship life of Reformed congregations. In this process, the place of the Prayer for Illumination was reasserted and at times held in tension with a recovery of the use of collects.

COLLECT OR PRAYER FOR ILLUMINATION?

Further liturgical developments within the Reformed tradition demonstrate a primary commitment to Calvin's vision of the Prayer for Illumination. However, there remained a historic interest in the traditional Roman understanding of the collect. During the twentieth century, worship books for Reformed churches adopted various approaches to the question of the place of the collect and/or the prayer for illumination in the liturgy. Barkley comments on the different approaches to the prayer for illumination between the Scottish, English, Welsh, and Irish rites. The Irish rite maintained a place for the collect as well as prayer for illumination before the reading of Scripture. By contrast,

> In the Scottish, English, and Welsh rites the prayer for illumination is placed before the sermon, but surely illumination is also necessary in the lections. The readings as well as the sermon, as Calvin maintained, are proclamation of the Gospel. That is why the prayer for illumination, as with Bucer and Calvin, ought to come not simply before the sermon, but before the readings and the sermon as a unity, and so within the preparation.[32]

Since the time of the *Westminster Directory*, the liturgical order had been complicated by the tendency for the sermon to move later in the service. This movement, however, did create the possibility for a recovered use of prayers in the opening rite in the *Book of Common Order* in 1940 in the Church of Scotland. In this order, a call to prayer (according to the seasons of the church year) is followed by a collect for purity which precedes

---

32. Barkley, *Worship of the Reformed Church*, 33.

the confession and pardon.[33] In these services, the prayer for illumination maintains a place before the sermon much later in the service.

The recognition of the historical and theological distinction between the Roman collect and the Prayer for Illumination is recognized in the development of new worship resources for Presbyterian churches in the United States. The provisional rites in the Service for the Lord's Day included the option of a prayer for illumination or a collect for the day following the *Gloria in Excelsis* and preceding the reading of Scripture. The commentary on this proposed order of worship noted:

> Though a prayer for illumination is in keeping with our Presbyterian tradition, some congregations may prefer to use the collect for the day prior to the reading of Scripture. The collect for the day is customary in many churches. *The Book of Common Worship* will provide such collects for each Lord's Day and for the special days and seasons of the Christian year.[34]

The publication of the *Worshipbook* in 1970 included a full set of collects for Sundays and feast days throughout the church year. The outline of the service, though, shows a continued Reformed preference for the Prayer for Illumination.[35]

RECENT DEVELOPMENTS

With the publication of the *Book of Common Worship* (BCW) in 1993, the Presbyterian Church (U.S.A.) moved further to make room for both a collect and a prayer for illumination as part of the Service for the Lord's Day. The provisional rites followed the direction of the *Worshipbook* by listing a prayer for illumination *or* the "prayer for the day" immediately preceding the reading of Scripture. However, an option is also included for the use of the prayer for the day as part of the praise and adoration in the opening

33. Hurlbut, *Liturgy of the Church of Scotland*, 109. Note that this order resembles none of the previous liturgies since it inserts the form(s) of collect(s) before the confession and pardon. Thus, the possibility of the collect returns, but not as a conclusion of the opening rite.

34. Presbyterian Church (U.S.A.), *Service for the Lord's Day*, 27–28.

35. The listing of the service includes the Prayer for Illumination as part of "The Basic Structure" and the Collect for the Day as an "Addition or Variant Form." Presbyterian Church (U.S.A.), *Worshipbook: Services*, 21.

movement of the rite (immediately following a call to worship).[36] By the time of the publication of the BCW, the liturgical landscape for the collect had once again shifted. The Prayer for Illumination is firmly returned to its original place before the reading of Scripture, after the completion of the Gathering/Opening Rite. However, the "Prayer of the Day" or an Opening Prayer is included immediately following a call to worship. The description of the service also notes that, "The prayer of the day may be used later in the service, for example, as the concluding collect to the prayers of the people," which occur after the sermon.[37]

Similar tendencies and tensions between the use of a collect (prayer of the day) and a prayer for illumination can be found in Reformed bodies in other parts of the world. *The Book of Divine Services* for the Presbyterian Church in Cameroon maintains the place of the prayer of the day in its historic location in the Roman Mass (at the close of the opening rite) while adding a prayer for illumination immediately preceding the sermon.[38]

In Germany, a new worship book for Reformed congregations provides three options for the Lord's Day Service:

> Form One—Prayer for Illumination as optional at the close of the gathering rite and before the reading of Scripture;
>
> Form Two—Prayer for Illumination at the close of the gathering rite;
>
> Form Three—Prayer of the Day at the close of the gathering rite[39]

These variations in form underscore the continued tension within various Reformed constituencies to both honor historical and liturgical distinctions while at the same time remaining open to ecumenical influences.[40]

36. Presbyterian Church (U.S.A.), *Service for the Lord's Day,* 26. Note once again, though, that while a collect returns to the opening part of the rite that it is placed in a new location in the order of service.

37. Presbyterian Church (U.S.A.), *Book of Common Worship,* 35.

38. *Book of Divine Services,* vol. 1, 4–5. It is worth noting that the book includes a prayer of the day and a prayer for illumination for each Sunday and feast day.

39. Bukowski, *Reformierte Liturgie,* 34–35. The rubrics following the Prayer of the Day are helpful to note: "Das *Kollektengebet* fast den Eröffnungs- und Anrufuungsteil zusammen und führt—mit der Bitte um das rechte Hören—zum Verkündigungsteil hin. Es schließt mit einer erkenbarren Formel, damit die Gemeinde mit 'Amen' einstimmen kann" (46).

40. A similar tension between the use of collects and prayers for illumination can be found in the resources of the Presbyterian Church in Korea. *The Book of Common Worship for the Presbyterian Church in the Republic of Korea* describes the prayer for illumination very briefly with a suggested placement before the sermon (51). Collects,

CONCLUDING OBSERVATIONS

In some ways, many within the Reformed Church have gone full circle in the treatment of the collect, while in other ways they continually redefined its place and use. What began in Strasbourg and Geneva in the sixteenth century continues to hold sway. As we have seen, the transformation of the collect into a prayer for illumination was a liturgically bold and theologically decisive act that reoriented the liturgy while still maintaining the traditional space for this prayer, but allowing it to point in a completely new direction. Here again the primary theological watchword of the Reformed church was influential, *Ecclesia reformata, semper reformanda*, "'the Church reformed, always to be reformed according to the Word of God' in the power of the Spirit."[41] The movement between form and freedom, central to the life and practices of Reformed congregations, brought ongoing liturgical change as Reformed churches worked to establish their theological and liturgical identity. In this regard, the study of the history of the collect in the Reformed Church provides insight into far more than one brief prayer; it foreshadows the broader liturgical history of Reformed congregations.

---

mostly based on the lectionary and some Korean church historical occasions, may be used in other parts of the service for the call to worship, litanies of thanksgiving, and litanies of confession (Part I. Sunday worship, 95–201).

41. See Presbyterian Church (U.S.A.), *Constitution of the Presbyterian Church (U.S.A.)*, F-2.02.

2

Calvin's Use of the Law and Christian Formation

LOOKING BACK OVER THE past fifty years, one can trace the results of liturgical renewal through the effects of Vatican II for both Roman Catholics and Protestants. Among other things, Vatican II inspired a renewed focus on the liturgical year, a common lectionary, a concerted effort to balance the role of word and table, and increased attention to the role of Christian formation. For Roman Catholics, a recovery of the ancient practices of the catechumenate became an important and central way to address the need for baptismal preparation for adults. The Rite of Christian Initiation of Adults (RCIA) offers a series of ritual stages for those preparing for baptism through periods of prayer, reflection, study, and discernment.

In this chapter, I explore ways that the rites of the catechumenate could be adapted within the framework of a Reformed perspective. How can one begin to learn and practice lessons from the catechumenate within the Reformed tradition where liturgical texts are neither fixed nor required? What I hope to show are possible ways that one aspect of the catechumenate could be adapted within the Reformed liturgy and insights that our Reformed approach might be able to offer our ecumenical partners. My plan in exploring this path is to suggest how other liturgical and confessional traditions might benefit from asking questions about the movement of the liturgy and exploring the ways that it may connect to the lifelong process of Christian spiritual formation.

One of the remarkable things about the catechumenate is the way that it challenges all of us to reassess how we approach questions of Christian identity and spiritual formation. Twenty years ago, as a pastor of a congregation struggling to find new life, my discovery of the catechumenal process came as a kind of lifeline to help me and the elders/leaders in our congregation reconsider our approach to Christian formation and congregational renewal. I was especially impressed with a small book by Alan Kreider, *The Change of Conversion and the Origin of Christendom*, which described the ancient practices of the catechumenate through the language of behaving, believing, and belonging. At the same time that the catechumenate and RCIA opened up new possibilities for me to raise questions about what it means to follow Jesus, it also pushed me back to theological resources in my own tradition. It is a bit of this dialogue that I want to share: a conversation between the documents of the RCIA and the theology of John Calvin that I offer as a way to challenge us to expand our vision, vocabulary, and practices of baptismal life. I will focus especially on the role of the scrutinies during the catechumenal process since it is during this process that baptismal candidates are expected to examine their lives in the midst of their community in order to ascertain their readiness to participate in the baptismal rites.

PART 1—THE ROLE OF THE SCRUTINIES

We begin this task by looking at baptismal preparation during the season of Lent. In the official liturgies of the RCIA, the scrutinies are described as part of the rites belonging to the period of purification and enlightenment. For three weeks, the baptismal candidates experience the movement between blessing and exorcism as central to their final preparation for baptism at the Easter Vigil. In the words of the RCIA, "the scrutinies are meant to uncover, then heal all that is weak, defective, or sinful in the hearts of the elect; to bring out, then strengthen all that is upright, strong, and good ."[1] The scrutinies provide the proscribed way in which those who are preparing for baptism will go through this final process of examination and repentance. In a carefully and thoughtfully constructed series of liturgies over the course of three weeks, the preparation of the baptismal candidates is coordinated with the lectionary readings from the Gospel of John about the Samaritan woman, the man born blind, and the raising of

1. *Rite of Christian Initiation of Adults*, 86.

Lazarus. These readings were chosen to point the candidates to Christ, who is the way, the truth, and the life. Building on the images of these texts, the rite of the scrutinies "should complete the conversion of the elect and deepen their resolve to hold fast to Christ and carry out their decision to love God above all."[2]

While there is much to appreciate and learn from the way that these liturgies are written and embodied, let me point out three critical questions that I want to explore from my own perspective as a Presbyterian.

First, why would one use language of purification and enlightenment, especially for this part of the process? It seems to me that using these words runs the risk of making baptismal preparation an end in itself rather than pointing to the ongoing process of regeneration that is central to the life of Christian faith. Instead, the implication seems to be that when one has reached a certain point of purity or a certain state of enlightenment then one is ready for baptism, which then ironically becomes something between an affirmation or at best a culminating point on this journey to the baptismal font.

Second is a question of agency: what is the source of the work that is done in this process of baptismal formation? Here, the language of the RCIA suggests that the rites themselves are responsible for producing the results in the lives of the baptismal candidates. To read this generously, surely it is an embodied understanding of the rites where the candidates gather with the presider while surrounded by the congregation. As a teacher and student of ritual, let me quickly note that I share a commitment to the power of rituals to change our lives. Nevertheless, let me suggest that it does matter where and how we name the power of transformation in our lives. Here, those of us who follow the catechumenate will benefit from clearly locating and articulating the Spirit as the sole source of our life in Christ. It is the Spirit at work in our stammering words, our sometimes clumsy gestures, and in our less than perfect communities, the Spirit who breathes new life on us, through us, and into us.

Thirdly, what is the role of the assembly in this process? In her brief description of the scrutinies, Roman Catholic catechumenist Diana Macalintal offers the following description: the scrutinies are "for the elect, not for the baptized. The baptized are no longer enslaved by Satan. Those who have not yet entered the waters of the font are still vulnerable; they have not yet been clothed with Christ; they have not yet been reborn as

2. *Rite of Christian Initiation of Adults*, 86.

new creations. That is why those who have already been released from the devil's grip are able to pray these scrutinies and exorcisms for the elect."[3] In response, I want to point not only to the role of the Spirit as the one who brings life to the assembly, but to the ongoing formation in Christian living that remains a regular and continuous part of the assembly's life together. Here, the liturgy extends a call to all of us to move forward into our life in Christ. Thus, I want to approach the process of baptismal formation and baptism itself as a communal call to renewal in which the Spirit stirs within us, not because of any particular status that we bring (as ones who have reached a level of purification or enlightenment) but solely by the grace of God.

PART 2—FORMATION FROM A REFORMED PERSPECTIVE AND CALVIN'S THIRD USE OF THE LAW

What is at stake in these deliberations are particular understandings of Christian identity and spiritual formation. To show an alternative portrait to the one that underlies the scrutinies, I want to examine two central aspects of Calvin's reflection on the process of Christian life and growth around two central themes: the role of the Law; and its relationship to the ongoing process of Christian growth or sanctification.

Calvin on the Role of the Law

While Martin Luther noted the role of the law in convicting us of sin and establishing a civil order, others during the time of the Protestant Reformation, such as Phillip Melanchton and the authors of the *Book of Concord*, added a third use of the law. John Calvin picked up this idea and expanded on it in his classic theological work, the *Institutes of the Christian Religion*.

Briefly, what are these three uses of the law? Calvin describes the first use of the law as a mirror that is designed to show us our sin and lead us to the covenant. Here, the understanding of the law's role follows Luther's understanding of the law as that which allows us to see our need for God's grace. The second use of the law provides a foundation for moral order. For example, Calvin used the Commandments in his time to guide the civic order of the city of Geneva. The third use of the Law is as a moral guide to

3. Macalintal, "History of the Scrutinies," 3.

support a distinctive kind of spirituality: a cultivation of piety.[4] Calvin des-
ignates this third use of the law as the "primary use of the law" as it points
out "the goal throughout life we are to strive."[5] In this context, the Law
continues to teach and urge us to do good and live in holiness. It functions
in this way because the Law serves as the "best instrument" for learning
God's will and as a guide for believers to live a life of gratitude.

It is critical to note that the language of the Law is not confined solely
to the Decalogue/Ten Commandments. Instead, Calvin understood the
Ten Commandments to exemplify God's revelation, promise, and covenant
with God's people. In this sense, the Ten Commandments represent God's
witness and presence to the people of the covenant. To quote Calvin: "I
understand by the word 'Law,' not only the Ten Commandments which
set forth a godly and righteous rule of living, but also the form of religion
handed down by God through Moses . . . to remind them of the covenant
made with their fathers, to which they are heirs."[6] Theologian Serene Jones
describes this definition of the Law as an "acclaimed portrait that presents
to us a vision of the godly life. The law is an aesthetic space—a portrait of a
life."[7] The Law presents us with images of life that are filled with beauty and
goodness. For Calvin, who interprets the Law in relationship to the covenant that is given to the children of Israel and handed down to the heirs
of the covenant, this is a broad vision of life in a community of the faithful.

For Calvin, this was not simply an abstract theological argument. It
was central to the way that he pictured and nurtured congregational life.
This expansive understanding of the Law is evident in the ways that it was
used and adapted in the liturgies of Reformed congregations. Let me note
a few of the options that we can find beginning with Calvin and extending
through the history of Reformed worship that show the relationship of the
Law to a particular understanding of spiritual formation that is grounded
in our baptisms.

1) Calvin's own liturgies demonstrate a kind of flexibility in terms of
ways that his third and primary use of the law is placed and embodied in
the liturgy.

In the Strasbourg liturgy, the Decalogue was sung following the Confession and Pardon. The congregation sang the first five Commandments

4. Gerrish, "Place of Calvin," 298.

5. Calvin, *Institutes* 2.7.13

6. Calvin, *Institutes* 1.7.1. Cited by Jones in "Glorious Creation, Beautiful Law," 33.

7. Jones, "Glorious Creation, Beautiful Law," 33.

which were followed by a prayer by the minister that God's will made known through the law "may also be inscribed and impressed upon our hearts."[8] After the prayer, the congregation sang the second table of the Commandments. Historian Bard Thompson notes that: "Here he [Calvin] employed the Law according to its 'third and principal use': not to accuse and convict the sinner (in which case the Commandments would likely precede a Confession of sin) but to bring the penitents to true piety by teaching them the will of God and exhorting them to obey. 'In this way the saints must press on' (Institutes 2.7.12)."[9]

In the Genevan liturgy, on most Sundays, the Decalogue was replaced by a psalm sung by the congregation following the Confession and Pardon. However, on Sundays when Communion was celebrated, a sung version of the Commandments replaced one of the Psalms. Before 1562, the Commandments were sung following the Prayer of Confession, whereas beginning in 1562, the commandments are sung following the Apostles' Creed and prior to the Communion Prayer.[10] In his description of the components of an order of worship, Calvin notes the importance of the Commandments as that which are given by God, and which "are applied at Baptism."[11] Here the theological link for Calvin is clearly in terms of covenant and dependence upon the grace that God bestows on us to live in right relationship in a covenantal community.

Similarly, the liturgy prepared by Calvin's follower John Knox and adopted by the Church of Scotland followed the Genevan model of confession and pardon followed by a sung psalm. It is worth noting, though, that the role of the Commandments is underscored in one of the Confessions of Sin provided in the liturgy. The confession begins with an acknowledgment of the covenant and the commandments as that which shows God's mercy, which is apparent both through the Law and through Jesus Christ.[12]

---

8. Thompson, *Liturgies of the Western Church*, 191.

9. Thompson, *Liturgies of the Western Church*, 191.

10. Calvin, *Writings on Pastoral Piety*, 111–12. The pattern of linking the commandments with the celebration of communion continued in Reformed congregations. For example, *Book of Common Worship* in 1946 includes a service entitled "The Commandments" which is recommended for use as a "separate service, or as introduction to Holy Communion, or with Morning or Evening Worship." *Book of Common Worship*, 115.

11. Calvin in La Maniere et Fasson in Thompson, *Liturgies of the Western Church*, 217.

12. Knox, *Liturgy of John Knox*, 98.

Recent Reformed liturgies have followed and expanded on this approach. In the Presbyterian Church (U.S.A.), the last two worship books have outlined complimentary roles for the commandments while also pointing to Calvin's broader understanding of Law. The Ten Commandments are paired with the summary of the law from Matt 22:37–40:

> Our Lord Jesus said:
> **You shall love the Lord your God**
> **with all your heart,**
> **and with all your soul,**
> **and with all your mind.**
> This is the greatest and first commandment.
> And a second is like it:
> **You shall love your neighbor as yourself.**
>
> On these two commandments
> hang all the law and the prophets.[13]

Both the Exodus and the Matthew texts are suggested as appropriate for preparation for worship as well as for use as an exhortation following the declaration of pardon. In addition, the new commandment of Jesus found in John 13 ("Hear the teaching of Christ: A new commandment I give to you, that you love one another as I have loved you")[14] is suggested for similar use.

Other Reformed bodies have ventured even further afield. For example, a liturgy from the contemporary French Reformed Church paraphrases Jesus' exchange with the rich young ruler from Mark 10 as the words of exhortation following a prayer of confession. Here, the emphasis is on the way the knowledge of the law and prophets takes shape in our lives. Jesus says to the man who asks about inheriting eternal life, "You know the commandments." The man responds that he has been keeping them since his youth. Jesus looks with love on him and says, "Sell what you own and give the money to the poor; then come, follow me."[15]

We can see from this example that the formative role of the Law cannot be understood separately from the good news of the gospel which invites us to celebrate the new life that God brings us. To summarize, Calvin's understanding of the law in general and particularly this third and primary use of the law refers not just to the Ten Commandments, but to the broader

13. Presbyterian Church (U.S.A.), *Book of Common Worship*, 29.

14. Presbyterian Church (U.S.A.), *Book of Common Worship*, 57.

15. *Liturgie de l'église Réformée de France*.

revelation of God that shows us as humans how to live in healthy relationships with God, our neighbors, and all of creation. It is closely connected to and embodied in Calvin's own liturgies and those of Reformed people over the past centuries. Calvin's theological commitment to the covenant and to the Law as central to God's revelation provides a foundation for his approach to spiritual formation and Christian identity.

Objections and Concerns

To be fair, Calvin's use and understanding of the Law has been contested by some theologians, particularly by Lutherans who worry that this approach to the Law runs the risk of compromising Luther's insistence on justification by faith. Does the appropriation of the Law (in any form) imply or support a form of works of righteousness or legalism that requires Christians to live up to certain standards in order to remain a part of the covenant community? What prevents us from confusing this third use of the law, to shape us in the image of Christ, with the first use, to convict us of our need for God?

Calvin offered a clever theological solution that anticipated these objections. His writings on Christian life point out a middle path between the Roman Catholic and Lutheran options of his day. Calvin accomplishes this by beginning his treatise on Christian life with a description of holiness (not as a call to perfection but as an encouragement to pious integrity). He anticipates Roman Catholic objections to his emphasis on justification by faith (which he shared with Luther) by pointing to the call to Christians to grow into our baptismal promises throughout our lives. This is also why Calvin flips the expected sequence of topics and presents them in the following order: sanctification, justification, and baptism. Here, the order is not chronological, but designed to show the deep interrelationship between these areas. Thus, for Calvin any theological discussion of baptism underscores the Christian commitment to a lifelong journey of discipleship.

In my opinion, a greater concern about the different uses of the Law is that of confusing the second use (to promote moral order) and third use of the law. Note how some Christian groups have adopted the practice of posting the Ten Commandments in public places as a way of supporting an understanding of Christendom. If we use the law in this way, then we will allow it to fulfill both its first and second functions: to provide for moral order and to convict those who are not identified with or have strayed from

Christian faith. In fact, this arose as a problem in the early history of the Protestant Reformation. Ornately decorated Roman Catholic churches were stripped of their images and altars. "In place of the altarpieces and statues that ornamented Catholic church in profusion, painted boards with the Ten Commandments and other biblical passages were the only decoration allowed in most Reformed temples."[16]

In his wonderful book entitled *Reconsidering John Calvin*, Randall Zachman, professor of Reformation studies at Notre Dame, describes this approach:

> The law, unfortunately, has now become a weapon to be used against others. In Indiana, there are many Christians who want to put the Ten Commandments everywhere because other people's lives are really screwed up, so if you just put the Ten Commandments out there then those people who are really messed up will get straightened out . . . . This approach is astonishingly naïve, but it is also outwardly directed, so that the law no longer awakens my conscience. We have learned how to use a mirror that was meant to lead us to descend into ourselves to see the deepest secrets we are concealing from ourselves and one another, so that it becomes a weapon we use against others, to tell other people to get their act in gear.[17]

Here is where the work of the catechumenate as formation into a new community offers an important word of correction to those of us in the Reformed community. It is not our task to construct or enforce a particular ideology, religious conviction, or way of life on our neighbors. Instead, the catechumenate helps us to recover the role of welcoming and learning to belong to an *alternative community* as fundamental to this shared way of Christian life. The catechumenate as a process of spiritual formation and discovery of gifts along with its rites and practices of belonging to a community provides an important model of what it may mean to share common Christian practices in these difficult political times in which we live. What we all share is a commitment that the goal of Christian formation is to make room for worship that shapes us as a community and as individuals to live in ways that show and demonstrate our reliance on God's grace. Or to use Calvin's own words: "The whole life of a Christian ought to be a sort

---

16. Description from Passwind in Benedict, *Christ's Churches Purely Reformed*, 497.

17. Zachman, *Reconsidering John Calvin*, 133.

of practice of godliness, because we have been called to sanctification."[18] On this central point, I believe that Calvin has another important message to offer us.

Calvin on Sanctification

In his description of Christian life, Calvin provides instructions in living for a rightly ordered life. Union with Christ allows us to live lives "infused with holiness." Note that for Calvin, "This union is not the goal, but the source of Christian life."[19] He describes holiness as part of the process of Christian life shared in community; this is the process of the Spirit's work in our lives and note that it is a distinctly different vision and placement in comparison to the language of purification found in the scrutinies. For Calvin, the purpose of Christian life is to live into the likeness of Christ. In his words, Christ "set before us as an example, whose pattern we ought to express in our life."[20] This teaching, which Calvin described in terms of doctrine, "must enter our hearts and pass into our daily living, and so transform us."[21] For Calvin, sanctification is not about reaching a level of perfection but about aspiring to live with integrity and thanksgiving.

On this very point, Calvin connects a vision of Christian life to his deep theological commitment that we belong to God. Here the law as God's vision and revelation of life in community (in all three of its uses) may serve as a source of guidance. As Calvin notes, "Thus, with reference to both tables of the Law, [God] commands us to put off our own nature and to deny whatever our reason and will dictate." This is a life described by Calvin in which we "travel as pilgrims in the world."[22]

Ultimately, though the primary action in terms of our participation in Christian life is depicted in Rom 12: that we present ourselves to God as a living sacrifice that we may be transformed by the Spirit's presence in our lives (note the possibility of parallels and difference here to the scrutinies).

To cite another favorite passage of Calvin's from 1 Cor 6:19: "We are not our own, we are God's;" Christian life then is the process of our lives

18. Calvin, *Institutes* 3.7.1, 685.

19. Horton, *Calvin on the Christian Life*, 105.

20. Calvin, *Institutes*, 3.6.2, 686.

21. Calvin, *Institutes*, 3.6.4, 688.

22. Calvin, *Institutes*, 3.7.3, 693. The footnote in this edition of *Institutes* notes that Calvin echoes the language of Augustine in the *City of God*.

being shaped in conformance to the One who has saved us. As Amy Plantinga Pauw notes, "the Reformed stress on sanctification is less an indicator of the success the church has had in achieving this holiness than it is a painful evidence of how much it needs the ongoing sanctifying work of the Holy Spirit."[23]

Calvin connects this vision of life as that which grows out of baptism: "Through the gospel a message of our cleansing and sanctification is brought to us; through such baptism the message is sealed."[24] Baptism provides a "cleansing for the whole of life." From the water of baptism, we emerge with a clear sense of devotion to God as a way of life. On this journey, we are guided by the rule of love to care for our neighbors and by the rule of gratitude: "When we are certain that the earthly life that we live is a gift of God's kindness, as we are beholden to God for it we ought to remember it and be thankful."[25]

PART 4—CONCLUSION: LESSONS LEARNED

While I previously noted a lesson that those of us in the Reformed community can learn from the catechumenate in terms of attempting to foist ideological expectations on our neighbors, let me close with three brief items which I believe that the catechumenate can learn from Calvin and the Reformed tradition. I offer these observations in the spirit and the language of the Leuenberg agreement, the Reformed and Lutheran document that calls us to signs of "mutual admonition and recognition."

We have the opportunity of creating a broader vision of the catechumenate. One of the fascinating and unexpected outcomes of this conversation is to note the common interest between Calvin's baptismal practice with its emphasis on communal worship and lifelong spiritual formation and that of the contemporary catechumenate. Both approaches have worked to recover a deeper and stronger vision of baptismal life. Here note even the important way that the change in language from an organization like the North American Association Catechumenate to the Journey for Baptismal Living shows a growing concern for an understanding of the catechumenate as a lifelong process. Careful language around our immersion

23. Pauw, "Graced Infirmity of the Church," 191.

24. Calvin, *Institutes*, 4.15.3, 1305.

25. Calvin, *Institutes*, 3.9.3, 715.

into Christian life at baptism as a source (rather than a goal) of Christian life will help avoid misunderstandings.

Let me point to a related, second outcome. Calvin's understanding of this broader, primary use of the Law as part of our shared liturgical life together offers an important corrective to the danger that the rites of the catechumenate will be interpreted in individualistic ways—as directed solely to the candidates coming for baptism. Instead the vision of our shared baptismal life draws us all together. All of the assembly gather to ask God's blessing on our shared journeys, on our discernment, on our practices, on our ongoing formation as disciples of Jesus Christ. Here the role of the community challenges the ways that the scrutinies can perceive to be directed to only a few. In an age of individualism, the church offers a vision of shared, communal life around word, water, and font.

Finally, to use Calvin's favorite words from the Apostle Paul: "We belong to God. We are not our own." This vision of Christian life looks to Christian formation as a lifelong journey that we share together. This vision of our life shared together is not based on our decisions or momentary capacity for self-denial or self-examination. Instead, this vision of the catechumenate grows out of the foundation of God's grace as the sole source of the Christian calling and life that we share together. The recovery of the catechumenate which has expanded our understanding of formation for baptism has much to gain by expanding its vision of formation to embrace the life that we celebrate together in and beyond the baptismal waters as the life that we share together as disciples of Jesus Christ.

3

The Historical Development of the Season of Easter

Lessons for Liturgical Renewal[1]

THE DEVELOPMENT OF EASTER as a fifty-day season in the church year was an extended historical process that allowed key theological themes to find their place as a part of this central celebration in the life of the church. Careful attention to the embodiment of these themes in our Easter celebration can foster the work of renewal in our own diverse communities of faith. A closer look at historical and theological factors that shaped the emergence of Easter as a liturgical season can provide insights to address the existential questions that many pastors sense as they lead worship.

Easter Sunday: The sanctuary is filling up while the brass section is warming up. The minister walks into the sanctuary to check on things one last time. A pitcher of warm water sits by the half-filled font, ready for the baptism of three infants and two adults.

The table is set with bread and wine. The Bible is marked and the sermon is ready to be preached. The minister is excited and weary from the services during the last three days—Maundy Thursday, Good Friday, and the Easter Vigil. He nods to the young man sitting in the second pew who was baptized last night. As he looks around the sanctuary, he recognizes many of the Easter Sunday visitors dressed in their new clothes. He has

---

1 This chapter was written with Cláudio Carvalhaes.

not seen many of them since the Christmas Eve service. He knows that for some of them, the service fills the time slot between the morning Easter egg hunt and the special brunch at the tennis club. As he looks around the sanctuary, he wishes that the celebration of Easter would be more than a social, cultural observance. He longs for the good news of the resurrection of Christ's body to take root in this sanctuary.

What will it take for the church to reclaim the Easter story and to live in light of it? Are there clues from the history of the church and from the work of liturgical scholars that can guide us to a more lasting and robust celebration of Easter that will nurture our Christian lives? In this article, we offer biblical and historical research on the development of the liturgical calendar and the lectionary as a basis for imaginative readings of ways in which diverse congregations in vastly different locations can reclaim the celebration of Easter as a season that shapes our faith.

HISTORICAL DEVELOPMENTS

In the early Jewish-Christian communities, the celebration of Easter began deeply rooted in its connection to the Passover calendar. From its inception, the celebration of Easter was connected to Jewish *seder* practices. In a review of first-century CE *seder* rituals, Larry Hoffman underscores the fluidity of practices that coexisted at the time. Hoffman characterizes the *seder* as "sacred theater" and outlines the rudimentary elements that were needed for the celebration: a table with food; open-ended questions to prompt conversation; a general (but not necessarily textual) rendition of Exodus 12; and a time of praising God, usually in the form of psalms.[2] Furthermore, Hoffman argues that Greco-Roman meal practice in the symposium provided a venue that gave shape to the *seder* which maintained an early emphasis on a shared meal and spontaneous conversation. Such a pattern served as a liturgical template for the development of Easter rituals while embedding them in practices that provided other layers of meanings.

The nature of early Christian celebrations of Easter has been characterized as unitive due to the association of resurrection with the broader account of Jesus' incarnation, life, and death. Kenneth Stevenson suggests that, "It would never have occurred to Christians living then to have had

---

2. Hoffman, "Passover Meal in Jewish Tradition," 13.

a Holy Week at all. For them it was sufficient to celebrate the death and resurrection of Jesus in one fell swoop."[3]

While scholars frequently use the language of the unitive nature of Easter to emphasize the way that it was inextricably connected to other services, this should not imply a uniformity to the assemblies' gatherings. Hence, the development of Easter practices can be seen as a complex merging of elements of the Greco-Roman banquet, Jewish *seder* practices, and the shared memories of Jesus' final days in Jerusalem.

Thus, even the language of Easter itself, known as *Pascha* (meaning passing through), began to carry a double memory of the Israelites' passing through the Red Sea in Exodus 12 as well as the story of Jesus' passing from death to new life. Through associative, typological, and figurative readings of Hebrew Scripture, Christian communities developed interpretations and ritual actions that further distinguished the Christian meal practices from those of their neighbors. Karl Gerlach demonstrates how homiletical reflections on Exodus 12 gave rise to narrative reinterpretation and ritualization within the context of a Christian assembly. Gerlach concludes, "As Christian authors view Exodus 12 as a narrative frame for stories about Christ and the Church, the paschal night provides a liturgical space for these stories to be told."[4]

Such a shift in ritual interpretation is accompanied by a growing controversy over the appropriate time for this celebration. For some Christian communities, the connection of the events of Holy Week to the celebrations of Passover (and their subsequent reinterpretation) required that the primary gathering coincide with the Jewish liturgical calendar which fixed the date as Nissan 14/15 (these communities were known as Quartodecimans

---

3. Stevenson, *Jerusalem Revisited*, 5.

4. Gerlach, *Antenicene Pascha*, 402. To cite but one example of this development, consider this excerpt from the paschal homily of Melito of Sardis from the late second century:

> [1] The scripture from the Hebrew Exodus has been read
> And the words of the *mystery* have been plainly stated,
> How the sheep (πρόβατον) is sacrificed
> And how the People is saved
> And how pharaoh is scourged through the *mystery*.
> [2] Understand, therefore, beloved,
> How it is new and old,
> Eternal and temporary,
> Perishable and imperishable,
> Mortal and immortal, this *mystery* of the Pascha . . .
> (cited in Gerlach, *Antenicene Pascha*, 62)

because of their allegiance to meeting on the fourteenth day of Nissan). Over time, other communities (for a variety of reasons) recognized the Sunday following Nissan 14/15 as particularly appropriate for the emphasis on Christ's resurrection, which was already a central theological rationale of the Sunday weekly assembly by Christians. The intense struggle over the differing dates for the celebration of Easter was one of the factors that prompted Constantine to call for the first ecumenical council in Nicaea in 325, which authorized the use of a Christian calendar to be followed by all churches.

J. Gordon Davies describes the liturgical developments around the celebration of Holy Week as characterized by a move from the symbolic to that of historical commemoration. The goal was to provide a model of the life of Christ that was accessible to the burgeoning numbers of Christians who joined the church in the post-Constantinian era.[5] According to Davies, the developments around the celebration of liturgical time in the fourth century served the primary purpose of providing a ritual narrative that invited participants to move through these accounts. A closer examination of the accounts of these celebrations suggests a more nuanced approach. While fourth-century celebrations of Holy Week in Jerusalem did make use of certain geographical locations (e.g., the Mount of Olives and Golgotha), other locations were surprisingly ignored. Paul Bradshaw notes that "no attempt was made to locate the Eucharistic celebrations on Holy Thursday at the supposed site of the Last Supper."[6] Stevenson refers to this development as "rememorative." History and symbolism are blended together in ways that make the rituals and narratives accessible to participants.[7] In the process, Easter began to take on its own emphasis.

Accompanying this transition was the growing tendency to associate baptism with Easter. At the end of the second century, Tertullian recommends Easter as a primary time for baptisms to occur. The ritual actions themselves provide a reframing and reinterpretation of biblical texts. A service that places the reading of Exodus 12 alongside baptism suggests links between the two that otherwise might likely go unnoticed. In his examination of homilies from ancient Syria, Gerlach notes the preferred status of baptismal typology in spite of attempts to develop eucharistic themes.[8]

5. Davies, *Holy Week*, 12–17.

6. Bradshaw, "Easter in Christian Tradition," 3.

7. Stevenson, *Jerusalem Revisited*, 9.

8. Gerlach, *Antenicene Pascha*, 405ff.

Increasingly, the celebration of a collection of unitive events around Jesus' death and resurrection that were marked in widely diverse ways in early Christian communities began to receive separate attention and were associated with particular occasions and designated services.

Over time, the increasing frequency of baptism as part of the celebration of Easter shaped Lent as a time of intense preparation for those who were presented as baptismal candidates. In some parts of the church where catechumens prepared for two to three years, the time leading up to their baptisms brought a heightened sense of anticipation.[9] The journals of Egeria provide a sketch of this process in Jerusalem in the fourth century CE.[10]

A more important development, though in terms of Easter as a liturgical season, was the designation of a series of services to reflect on one's baptismal experience following the Easter services. The acceptance and transformation of Pentecost from a Jewish harvest festival occurring fifty days after Passover by early Jewish and gentile Christian communities provided a period of time that took on increased importance. The book of Acts already portrays a theological reinterpretation of this festival by associating it with the emergence of the church as a result of the work of the Holy Spirit. Already by the second century CE, the Christian observance of Pentecost had moved in a distinctly different direction from its Jewish antecedents. Martin Connell notes, "Unlike the Jewish feast, which marked the day of Pentecost alone, the Christian practice, when it first appears, marked a quinquagesima, a period of 'fifty days' including and following the feast of Easter."[11] The shift in calendar to marking this lengthy period of time was accompanied by a shift in tone that focused on the days as a time of prolonged celebration with daily gatherings increasingly taking on Sunday practices, including a ban on fasting. These developments brought together a period of prolonged mystagogical reflection on baptism during the season of Easter with the theological notion of the church's birth celebrated on Pentecost as the culmination of the great fifty days. Craig Satterlee has chronicled this approach to post-baptismal reflection in his work on the sermons of Ambrose of Milan. "Thus, the purpose of mystagogical preaching was to 'explain' to the neophytes or newly baptized 'the meaning

---

9. A few recent attempts have picked up on this historic connection between Lent and baptism. For example, see Hall, "Becoming Christian."

10. See Wilkinson, *Egeria's Travels to the Holy Land*.

11. Connell, "From Easter to Pentecost," 94. Emphasis original.

and nature of the liturgical actions in which they have participated: baptism and Eucharist.'"[12]

Accompanying these developments in separating the paschal events into distinct festivals was the growing importance of pilgrimage especially to Jerusalem and the association of events with particular historical sites. Such a process leads Martin Connell to conclude:

> The span of the first five or six centuries of the Christian faith seems to indicate a general movement from the integrity of *qui-quagesima* to its dissolution in late antiquity and the early Middle Ages, perhaps as a result of the same tendency to historicize the life of Jesus of Nazareth in liturgical celebration that also brought Holy Week into being.[13]

In the midst of this process of liturgical adaptation, Anscar Chupungco has challenged us to note other influences at work. Chupungco underscores the cosmic claims of Easter and the theological possibilities of linking Easter to the cycles of nature. Following the spiritual and allegorical linking of spring with Christ's passion, Chupungco concludes that, "Easter is a spring feast in every respect, from its origin and development to its ritual expressions. As a result there is a kind of symbiosis between the Christian feast and springtime. The qualities of one have been absorbed by the other."[14] In churches in the northern hemisphere, the celebration of the season of Easter retains ties to the return of Spring and the renewal of the earth. By contrast, churches in the southern hemisphere experience these cosmic cycles in ways that the season of Easter becomes a promise to accompany them on the seasonal journey through fall and winter. From either perspective, it is important to note the development of Easter as it relates to our relationship to the earth.

Summary

These insights from the historical development of the season of Easter are presented in order to highlight certain theological themes that took place in different settings in the life of the early church: diverse ways of gathering around table, extending Easter as a season of fifty days, celebrating

12. See Satterlee, *Ambrose of Milan's Method.*
13. Connell, "From Easter to Pentecost," 105.
14. Chupungco, *Shaping the Easter Feast,* 36.

baptisms and reflecting on lives shared together, linking Easter with the rhythms of the earth. In light of this historical sketch, what follows are three imaginary narratives of the ways in which the celebration of the season of Easter could be marked today.

SCENES FROM CONGREGATIONAL LIFE

1. Congregational Rebirth in the US

When you ask any of the old-timers how new life came to Grace Presbyterian Church, they all point to the same starting place. It began the spring that there was a hole in the roof of the sanctuary. For years the congregation had been slowly declining. They had watched the neighborhood around the old church building change as well. Crime had increased and the old houses surrounding the church seemed to be decaying. Many of the members of the church moved out of the neighborhood to the suburbs and while some continued to drive in to the city for Sunday morning services, it looked to be only a matter of time until the church would close its doors for good. The congregation had tried adding new services and offering programs. They might work for a while, but they never seemed to last. As the congregation grew smaller and smaller, all they could do was to gather for the regular services. When torrential rain came that spring, a leak began in the sanctuary and threatened to change the place that they gathered for worship. So the congregation took the last of the church's endowment to pay a roofer to patch up the roof.

The roofer told them that he would start working on the roof during Holy Week and that the sanctuary would be closed. When the session began to plan the Good Friday service, they looked for a different place to meet. Given the changes that they were facing, their young pastors encouraged them to try something new. They would walk through the neighborhood and have a service of readings from the passion story at places where violence in the neighborhood had taken place during the last year. Amidst darkened skies, a small group of about twenty people met outside the old sanctuary at noon. They looked up towards the sky and saw the roofing crew pounding nails on the roof of the church building. Slowly they made their way to the street to the first gathering place. Late in December, a young boy had been killed by gunfire from a drive-by shooting while playing in his living room. The group from the church stopped in front of the house and began to sing, "Were you there when they crucified my Lord?" An elder read of Jesus praying in the Garden of Gethsemane. And then they moved on to the next stop. In front of a small grocery store, they gathered at the place where an older woman had been robbed. The force of the blow on her head had caused her to fall and she was injured so badly that she died several weeks later. Quietly the church group sang again, "Were you there when they crucified my Lord?" Tears filled their eyes as the gospel was read.

After two hours of walking through the neighborhood, they returned to the church. The group was tired, but they promised to meet for an Easter service on Sunday morning. When they gathered three days later, the pastor stood up and announced, "This morning, I have asked a few of our members to speak about the service we held on Friday." One by one, they talked about how deeply they were moved by what they had seen and felt as they walked around the neighborhood. Then the pastor spoke: "We cannot stay inside the walls of this church any longer. This morning we are unlocking the doors of this church and we are committing ourselves to working for justice in this community. May the Spirit of God breathe new life into us as we go forth. Christ is risen indeed. Alleluia!"

The change did not come about magically. Day after day, they gathered for a small meal and began to walk around the same streets of the neighborhood. On Fridays, they began serving a meal at the church for homeless people in the neighborhood. On Mondays, they worked in the community garden planting, watering, and weeding. On Wednesday afternoons, they volunteered as tutors in the elementary school. Every Saturday morning, they picked up the trash in the school yard down the street.

Starting that season of Easter, each Sunday service included reports on the church's involvement in the neighborhood and an open invitation to bring friends and neighbors to help with the work. At the end of each Sunday service, they gathered around the baptismal font and prayed for God to strengthen them and bless the work that had begun. Slowly, but surely, Grace Presbyterian Church began to grow.

2. Eucharist and Baptism during Easter Sunday in Mexico

It was Easter morning. After picking up people in various places around town, we traveled in two big vans for about two hours from Nogales into a small village in the countryside of Mexico. We arrived at a place where people were already waiting for us. The place was all decorated with colorful banners and handmade paper crafts. It was a piece of land with fruit trees, a small house with a room, a kitchen, and a bathroom where the pastor lived by himself, a large unfinished church building without doors or windows, and what seemed to be a small swimming pool. After being welcomed and sharing *la paz del Señor*, everybody started to prepare the fire and set the table in order to begin to eat. Tortillas and wine were placed among the food. At one point the pastor said: "*Oremos hermanos y hermanas*" and he prayed thanking God for that special day that we were celebrating the resurrection of Jesus Christ. After he prayed he said: "Today is special for us! As Christians we remember the life, death, and resurrection of Jesus Christ. And to celebrate that vividly, we are going to have the Lord's Supper and baptism! Around the table we eat and share the life of Christ and our lives together. . . *y no podemos nos olvidar de eso*" and he went on talking about the ways in which Christ transformed his own life. Then he said: "We are here because of Christ. . . remember that last night when Jesus ate with his disciples. . ." and he went on to say the words of institution, breaking the tortillas and pouring the wine. "*Mira, la comida de Dios para nosotros.*" He then shared the tortillas and the wine with all of us and we ate and drank around the table.

We continued our eucharistic meal now with fried chicken, tortillas, chili, tomato, lettuce, crema, and guacamole. Background music played and children, adults, and dogs were all fed. After we ate, we were called to sit under a tree instead of moving to the empty church building. We started singing as if the service was continuing without any break. Testimonies were offered, songs were sung, and several Bible passages were read. The pastor then preached, saying how important it was for us to get together on Easter day, because on that morning Jesus had resurrected and was alive and that day was very special. "*Tenemos que celebrar hermanos y hermanas! No death could hold Jesus down and Jesus' life is what keep us going. Vamos desde los días de los muertos hasta el día de los vivos.*" He also discussed how many times in our lives we die and resurrect and the fact that we were eating together on that very special day was because of Jesus' death and resurrection. "*No es verdad hermana Maria, no es asi mismo hermano Jorge?*"

He then started to talk about baptism as a new life out of death and how the Christian church around the world has always done that, how we become part of God's global family and how we now, through the love of God in Christ, have a deep sense of belonging. He invited us all to the tiny swimming pool and once we were all gathered there he said: "This water is our water reservoir. Here we pour the water that comes to us during the week and also save the water when it rains. But now, our water reservoir is going to be our baptismal font, our Jordan river where our brothers and sisters will be baptized. *Hay mucha agua para nosotros!* Our lives are marked by the waters of our baptism and the remembrance of our baptism sustain and continues to transform our lives. *Jesús es la agua de la vida hermanos y hermanas!"*

He knelt and, moving the waters with his hand, said: "Through the waters God seals us with God's love, and today we remember this love in Jesus' death and resurrection for us." He stood up and brought one candidate at a time into the water. There, with the help of two deacons, he asked questions pertaining to the candidate's faith. After that they were immersed in the water and when they came out, there was an explosion of claps and praises among the community with people shouting: *"Gracias a Dios que esta vivo, somos una familia!"* After the candidates were baptized, we sang a song and a baptismal certificate was given to each of the new members. During this, the pastor said: "when you go to the consulate to get your visa to go to the United States, they will ask for your birth certificate. Now you can bring your baptismal certificate because they will accept it too. You are now born into God's love and belong to God's family." We prayed and sang once more while the new members received hugs from everybody. We sang *Pues si vivimos, para el Señor vivimos, somos del señor, somos del Señor.* The pastor invited us back to the table to continue eating while the kids went to the water reservoir/baptismal tank that now became their swimming pool. Then the pastor blessed us by saying: "Brothers and sisters, what a joyful day today. We ate together, we celebrated Jesus' life, death, and resurrection and we participated in the baptism of our family members. Now, our kids are playing in the water. The water of our baptism is the water of our lives, the waters that quench our thirst, that wet our lands and give us food, that give us life, joy and new life. This Easter, let us remember that we belong to the water, gift of God to the world, and through the waters of our baptism, we belong to Jesus Christ, gift of God to the transformation of the world. Go in peace under God's resurrected son, preserve the water, and keep your faith, Amen."

3. Eucharist and Pilgrimage in Guatemala

It was Easter day. The church was getting filled at six o'clock and there was incense wafting around this church made by indigenous people from Guatemala. People were gathering at the sanctuary and making conversation as they prepared for the service. Children were already running around playing with each other. The band got into their space and people started to wind down their conversations. A man came to the microphone and said: "*Buenos días hermanas y hermanos.* We are here today very early in the morning to remember the day when the women went to Jesus' tomb just to find out that the tomb was empty. Alleluia! We are here at this Easter Sunday to celebrate that the tomb is empty, that the women saw Jesus resurrected, and that Jesus won over death forever. Praise be to God!" He prayed and invited people to sing.

After a time of singing hymns and coritos, people sat down and the pastor started to preach from the pulpit: "*Hermanos y hermanas*, in the midst of the life that Jesus gave to us, we must remember our brothers and sisters who died trying to cross the desert looking for a better life for their families. We must remember those who are still on their way and we haven't heard from them anymore. We must remember those who cannot come back and those who have no means to try a new life. We must remember the families that stayed here and are fractured by the absence of a mother, a father, a son, or are going through illness without means of being treated. As we remember Jesus Christ, the way he passed from life to death and back to life again, the Passover is very important for us too. Because like the Hebrews in Egypt, who were trying to find a promised land, we too are trying to pass-over the desert both ways to keep our families fed and alive. Sometimes the *crossing* of the desert for us is like the *cross* of Jesus Christ, crossing from death to life, being cross-ed by the wall, injustices and with a high price to pay. The sacrifice of Jesus becomes our sacrifice as we also try to search for more just ways to live. *Ai hermanos y hermanas*, we all belong to the *cross*-ing *cross*-er life of Jesus Christ! Let us not forget that Easter was only possible because of Good Friday! So, if you are cross-ing the desert alone or with your family in the future, among bandits and robbers and drug-dealers, don't forget that we must keep the promise of Easter and the hope of a new life! Let us pray for all of those who are passing/crossing over places and doing it for the love of their families. Let us pray that God gives them and us, cross-er people, a promised land as well, be it here, in our pilgrimage or anywhere else."

He paused, breathed, and said "Let us pray . . ." As the church started to pray, the space was filled with loud prayers and soon, drowning tears. For about an hour, people prayed alone, then together, then alone again, standing, shouting, jumping up and down, crying, quietly on bent knees, supplicating God's mercy and favor towards them and their families. We could hear several people asking for children without fathers and mothers, and for those who were deported and had nothing else to do in their homeland; for kids who learned about gangs in the US and were deported to their countries and started violent gangs; for women raped and abused by coyotes and border patrol police along the desert. We would hear about split families, torn down by the lack of jobs, threatened by people who lend them money to *cross* the desert but had to come back home without any success, couples estranged for such a long time without seeing each other. The prayers made the building become heavy and after a while the movements started to slow down.

As the prayers started to lose intensity, people sat down and remained seated in the pews. A deep silence took over the worship space and the whole congregation didn't say a word or make a move. After what seemed to be a very long time, the pastor came to the eucharistic table and, assisted by two women, uncovered the bread and the wine for the Eucharist. The pastor said: "*Hermanos y hermanas, hay aqui alguno que quiera dar un testimonio?*" People were so tired that very surprisingly, silence was kept intact. From the table the pastor continued: "Don't give up! God has given us life! God has provided for the journey. Look and see, we have food for the journey! Especially at this Easter day, as we eat and drink this food, we *must* remember and never forget that life is bigger than death! No matter what you or your family are going through, or where you might be in your pilgrimage, there is promise of life for you to keep going. Today is the Easter of our Lord Jesus Christ and because of Jesus, it is our own Easter as well!

"Like the women who went to the tomb, we are called to go there and see that our Lord is risen! Let us keep going brother and sisters. We cannot stop or we will die before time like so many of our people! Here at this table are the signs and the promises of our new life, life always renewed to us. Like Jesus with his disciples and friends, it is the eating and drinking together that help us continue our journey. Here we stop and renew our strength, here we stop and find rest, here we stop and gain new perspectives, here we stop and are reminded that we are not alone, that God almighty is with us and that the church of Jesus Christ, God's family is with us, here in Guatemala, in El Salvador, in Honduras, in Mexico and in Estados Unidos.

"As we are about to eat this bread and drink this wine, remember the powerful life and death and resurrection of Jesus Christ. Jesus fought against the injustices of his time and was killed. Now, in Jesus' memory, get your portion of strength and renewal and transformation and go back to the road trusting that God in Jesus, through the work of the Holy Spirit will walk with you, will be part of your pilgrimage, and will give you a new Jerusalem, a promised land here and also when you die. See, we can still be thankful to God's love in our lives can't we? Let us do this: as you take a piece of this bread, give it to somebody else and receive it from somebody else as a gesture of our life together, of our dependence on each other, as a reminder that we are not alone and that is here in our midst through each other." And raising the bread he said, "On the night when Jesus had his last supper with his friends. . ."

CONCLUSION

These figurings of the church of Jesus Christ in different places shows the diversity of situations where people are celebrating Eucharist, each place with its own specificity and with a different understanding of the season of Easter. Since its inception, Easter is the weaving of God's story in our story, and our story reshaped by the story of God. Easter is not an isolated event but a culmination of present, past, and future of God's presence in history. At Easter, creation is reclaimed, our past is redone, our present is firmly grasped, and our future holds a promise. During Easter, we celebrate not only Jesus' resurrection but also Jesus' life and death, because resurrection only makes sense in light of the ethical ways Jesus lived his life. In Christ, Easter becomes a political project for the world, as it embraces the world with prophetic admonitions and the promise of transformation.

Grace Presbyterian Church finds a way back when they reach out to others. The repetitive signs of a dwindling church has its claws deeply entrenched in their souls and a sense of helplessness carries the scent of death. However, it was Easter time that provided new life for this congregation. Instead of ending in the cemetery, their journey took on another route and new life came upon them. Where there was death, now there is a stubborn sense of newness.

The Mexican Baptist church shows us that life is interconnected in deep ways. No compartmentalization of the congregation, no separation between Christian education, testimonies, drinking water, baptism and fun, preaching, the pastor's house, the worshiping tree, tortillas, guacamole, crema, grape juice, hymns, coritos, and life. In this community, drinking water became the baptismal font as a way into Easter and then back to the place of play for children who are nurtured by the community. Citizenship and baptism are understood as the same and the nation-state and church family are closely connected, for better or for worse. Easter time is about families connecting, new people joining, and the world gathered around the dining table and the baptismal font/reservoir/pool.

The Guatemalan Pentecostal church seems to be the only place where people can go and feel the world as bearable. The weight of disgrace crushing people's lives is so pervasive that life is always at risk of being taken away in a heartbeat. In the midst of death, of rupture, of brokenness, Easter is this "brute flower of desire"[15] that forces life into the midst of these people, who instead of nihilism choose the painful path of believing that life is still stronger than death. In a world that forbids them the luxury of living simply with their families, that does not allow them to live with a minimum assurance of help or providence, that prevents them from moving, that insists on keeping them without social or economic choices, Easter becomes the place of safety, a country of radical belonging without borders and walls where dreams of a just society and family reunion can be nurtured.

In these figurings of the churches of Christ in times of Easter, we can notice the following:

1. Easter goes from being a celebration on a given Sunday of the calendar to becoming a way of living. The development of celebrating Easter as a season of fifty days marks the understanding of Easter as not simply a point in time, but a journey on which we go. Ultimately, Easter saturates the entire liturgical calendar and life as it is repeated every Sunday. No matter when we are celebrating, it will always be Easter.

2. Yet, Easter never comes without the wrestlings of life and the brutalities of Good Friday. The early historical celebration of Easter held closely to the inherent relationship between death and life. Sundays arrive only after the announcements of death along the way, the Tenebrae of Wednesdays, the anguishes of Maundy Thursdays, the desperation of

15. Caetano Veloso, "O Quereres," in *Personalidade*, Polygram, 1993.

Good Fridays, the numbness and revolt of Saturdays. Then and only then, are we able to figure out what Easter Sunday is all about.

3. Easter links together a basic sacramental pattern for the life of the church. A meal gathering and the welcoming of new brothers and sisters through the waters of baptism are basic to the Easter celebration.

4. Easter then provides a framework to live in the world by the ways in which Christ lived: There is the proclamation of a new and alternative way of living in God's kingdom, with the beatitudes, the parables, the harsh demands to love your neighbor, to share food, feelings, and belongings with those excluded. This new way of living is always pressing against injustices, class divides, and the status quo. Even if our culture has made Easter a cultural event, tamed from the challenges and exigencies that Easter entails, we are nonetheless required by Easter to pay attention to the things God and God's kingdom requires of us that were demonstrated in the life of Jesus.

5. Easter brings a sense of becoming, not only in a figurative way but very concretely: it starts social processes, it reunites people, it hinders evil, it teaches us to share our belongings and to pay attention to someone else's life. We are required to offer help, presence, means, and tools to our brothers and sisters who wrestle with whatever is at stake in their lives.

6. Easter prompts people to probe for a sense of gratitude and to offer thanksgiving as a way of maintaining balance with the difficulties of life.

7. Easter is about a "dangerous and liberating memory"[16] of Jesus that becomes a source of continuous hope and social transformation for all and especially for the crucified people.

8. Easter is the unbelievable promise and possibility of life in a world where death spreads everywhere.

16. "*memoria passionis, mortis, et resurrectionis Jesu Christi. . .* a dangerous and liberating memory, which badgers the present and calls it into question. . .[and] compels believers to be in a continual state of transformation in order to take this future into account." Metz, *Faith in History and Society*, 88–89, emphasis original.

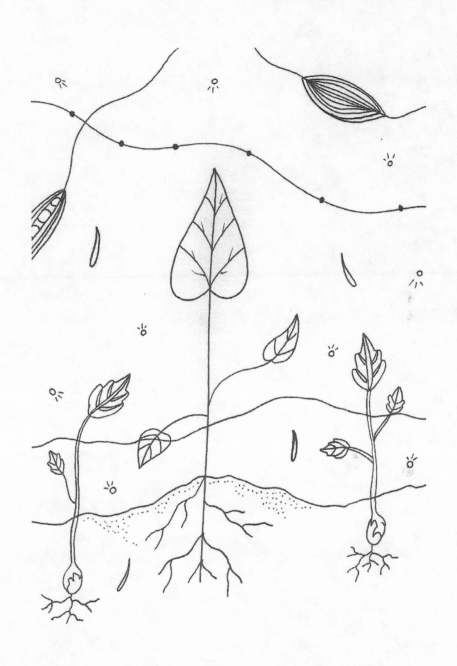

PART TWO

Present Experiences

WORSHIPING COMMUNITIES GATHER AROUND Word and Sacrament. Calvin understood these events to be the defining marks of the church as the place where the word is rightly preached and heard, and the sacraments are duly administered. As we observed in the opening section of this book, the interpretation of Scripture and the celebration of the sacraments has happened in diverse ways throughout the history of the church. There simply is no straight line between ancient Galilee and modern Galveston. Instead, the gospel is inculturated both in terms of the ways that we read and interpret Jesus' teaching as well as in terms of the ways that practices of initiation and meals are enacted and embodied in our communities. While ecclesial bodies and denominations have sought to establish norms for their communities, these parameters have primarily provided a form of porous boundaries around what some view as "proper" or "authorized" ways of preaching and presiding. To cite but one example, note the attempt by the Roman Catholic Church in the fourth century to control the practice of Eucharist by legislating that only bread, water, and wine are allowed during the celebration of the Mass. What a rule of this nature suggests is: a) other elements have been part of the eucharistic celebration in some communities; and b) while legislation can be passed, it may be much more difficult to enforce conformity across large geographical areas.

Reformed communities have largely avoided attempts to prescribe specific words, gestures, and ways that ministers are required to preach and celebrate the sacraments.[1] In place of detailed rubrics, a historic emphasis on the role of form and freedom provided a common framework for practice, discussion, and debate. In terms of preaching, the theological emphasis on the role of the Spirit serves as a foundation for the proclamation of the Word as an event in which the community gathers to encounter the claims of the text upon our lives. The work of the Spirit is integrally connected to the historical emphasis on the preparation and training of the clergy who bear the responsibility to exegete biblical texts in ways that draw on the methods of scholarship at any given time. As any seminary student quickly learns, though, sermons are not exegetical lectures on particular texts. Instead, the proclamation of the gospel occurs at an intersection where listeners encounter the claims of a biblical text on our lives. Here, the role of the preacher is to proclaim a message so that through the work of the Spirit, listeners may hear and live out the claims of the Gospels on our lives in ways that undergird our baptismal identity as followers of Jesus Christ.

Similarly, for Reformed Christians the absence of fixed, required liturgical texts and gestures in the celebration of baptism and Eucharist underscores a theological commitment to the sacraments as grace-filled events that take shape on our bodies as we gather around Word, water, bread, and wine. It is interesting to observe the ways in which Reformed leaders have understood and articulated the shared experiences of the proclamation of the Word and yet have often overlooked the formative ways in which the celebration of the sacraments provides a way to perceive the world around us. Note, for example, the historic importance of reading Scripture as a daily devotional practice that extends the lessons of Scripture into our daily lives versus the tendency to see the sacraments primarily as spiritual moments defined by the church and belonging to it. Thus, while Reformed communities sought to escape what they understood as hierarchical, legislative approaches through which the church controlled the sacraments (and in some times and places marketed them for their soteriological value), nevertheless Reformed approaches largely ignored and lost the benefit of the broader sacramentality that undergirded the broader catholic (with a small "c") tradition.

The pressing, present need, then, is to articulate Reformed practices that address the hopes and goals of communities as we gather around Word and Sacrament. The following chapters explore ways that preaching and

1. The requirement for the Words of Institution has been the one historic exception in terms of a required text for the Lord's Supper.

the celebration of the sacraments provide opportunities to shape our understanding and practice of Christian discipleship. The first two chapters examine the formative role of preaching in two significant ways: 1. the increasing importance of the role of preaching in terms of nurturing biblical literacy in the life of the congregation; and 2. showing the way that preaching helps create a sacramental imagination for the community of faith. The first of these essays examines options that preachers have in terms of the ways in which they approach the task of interpretation. In this task, the preacher approaches the sermon as a chance to model key perspectives on Christian faith via an encounter with biblical texts. The second essay shows ways in which the liturgical context opens up the space so that we experience texts in light of the elements and experiences that surround it. Here the reading and hearing of texts alongside the embodied actions at the baptismal font and the communion table challenge other interpretations of texts and help create a sacramental imagination that challenges the ways in which we see the world around us.

The following two chapters study the language and patterns of the celebration of the sacraments in order to ascertain ways in which they provide patterns for our daily lives. The goal is to tease out ways in which we can intentionally develop a sacramental ethic that helps us orient and experience our daily lives in light of our experiences at the font and table. Clarifying these practices is an important step on the Reformed road to recovering a genuinely catholic sacramentality.

Together, these chapters portray and critique the ways in which our current communal practices around Word and Sacrament foster particular forms of spirituality that nurture our identity as Christians. This section lays out steps that address the present ecclesiological crisis and preserve our commitment to the centrality of Word and Sacrament while opening up new possibilities for how this commitment takes shape in our lives.

4

Preaching as Building Biblical Literacy

While Vatican II highlighted the need for increased attention to the task of Christian formation for growth in the life of faith, it also included revolutionary changes to the Roman Catholic celebration of the mass. One of the outcomes championed by the liturgical renewal movement was the new focus on the role and active participation of the assembly. The reorientation of the service, with the priest now facing the congregation, brought a dramatic change to the eucharistic celebration. Accompanying this shift was a new focus on the centrality of Scripture and the role of preaching as central to the task of opening up the riches of Scripture.

Slowly, Protestants began to recognize the shifts in the Roman Catholic celebration of the Mass as a call for their own worship renewal. An important development was the adaptation of a common lectionary, a list of biblical readings recommended for use. The development of a new lectionary that began as a result of a renewed emphasis on biblical texts in the mass prompted Protestants to examine their own approach to the place of biblical texts within worship. The timing of these developments was fortuitous as they accompanied a period of scholarly emphasis on the development of a biblical theology and a focus on metanarratives that articulated a theology of salvation history. Like Roman Catholics, many Protestant churches were also dealing with increased concerns about biblical literacy in their congregations. In many ways, the new lectionary provided a road map by suggesting connections between texts and theological interpretations.[1] Along with

1. For example, note the way that the coordination of Old Testament texts to the gospel reinforces christological readings of Hebrew Scripture.

the development of a common lectionary, the increased use of the liturgical year among Protestant congregations privileged particular interpretations of biblical texts that supported ways of approaching Scripture as a presentation of salvation history. While Roman Catholics and Protestants continued to hold particular theological perspectives that differed, the work of liturgical renewal prompted them to recognize basic areas of commonality.

The rise of postmodern critiques of metanarratives opens up an opportunity for the church to reexamine the way in which Scripture prompts us to look at the world around us. In the words of the French philosopher Jean-Francois Lyotard, "Simplifying to the extreme, I define postmodern as an incredulity towards metanarratives."[2] From this perspective, there are significant questions about modern forms of biblical theology that propose foundational or over-arching themes as a basis for theological interpretation.[3] In light of this significant critique of biblical theology, are there other ways in which communities of faith can support the goals of Christian formation and biblical literacy that avoid the risks of forcing texts into theological frameworks with predetermined meanings? The challenges of the twenty-first century are pushing us to reexamine the basic question of how we deal with texts.

WAYS TO HEAR AND READ A TEXT

Slowly, the man pulled a large print Bible out of a plastic bag. He sat down next to me on a bench and carefully opened it up. The book was jammed full of scraps of paper marking well-worn pages throughout the Bible. He found the beginning and arduously began reading it to me. Word by word, syllable by syllable, he sounded out the words and spit them out into the hot, humid air: "In the beginning, God created heaven and earth."

He would read a phrase and then offer long words of explanation. Sometimes he spoke gibberish. Sometimes he passed on strange, archaic old formulas that he had learned in Sunday School. At times, he spewed disturbing racial and gender stereotypes that he had learned in church. But always, he returned to the book and to the slow process of reading out the words of the text. It was not simply that he read this book. This book read him. It defined his life and shaped his way of looking at the world. These

2. Lyotard, *Postmodern Condition*.

3. As an example, note the challenges to theology as *Heilsgeschichte* as an over-arching theological schema.

stories provided an interpretive lens for his efforts to try to come to grips with the world around him as well as to find resources for the turmoil and trouble of his own life.

I am haunted by images of watching this man read and interpret Scripture. On the one hand, his immersion into and engagement with Scripture provides a compelling and admirable model of grounding one's identity and worldview through the reading of the biblical text. On the other hand, his unquestioning acceptance of demeaning stereotypes is a troubling reminder of the ways that readers unconsciously interact with texts and use them to reinforce contemporary cultural biases and presuppositions.

It is worth noting that the development of the historical-critical method was precisely to challenge the dogmatic and doctrinal claims that were often being read into biblical texts. The rise of the historical-critical method sought to provide a methodology whereby the hermeneutical task had particular, objective tools in order to interpret texts. In the process, the historical-critical method often became captive to the elusive quest of historical certitude via investigations that searched for the original intent of an author. The rise of postmodernity has exposed much of the fragility of this task by uncovering the attempt to prescribe particular meanings onto texts.

In light of the renewed emphasis on the dynamic nature of interpreting texts, it is helpful to reframe our question in a way that underscores the interplay between reader and text: What is this Word and how does it shape and form us? In this era of information where we are continually bombarded with messages, advertising, scrolling data, news updates, and editorial interpretations, how do the words of Scripture still hold claim on us?

Sunday after Sunday, in some shape, manner, and form congregations gather to hear Scripture read and proclaimed. The preacher rises up and stands in the middle of the congregation to point to connections between these ancient texts and our lives. This intersection provides a base of orientation for the ways that the community sees faith at work in their lives. Sermons show the ways in which Scripture opens up new worlds. The theological world that we inhabit as a result of hearing these texts read and interpreted makes decisive claims on our lives. For example, I know a nun who spends one afternoon each week recording books for a blind school. She reads the texts carefully into a tape recorder and leaves behind these words for others to hear. She never sees the results of what she does—the way that these recordings sound in the ears, the ways that they shape the lives of those who hear them, or the vistas that these texts open up in the lives of the listeners. But it is enough for her to know that her voice brings these texts to life for those who otherwise might not have access to them.

I am often surrounded by books. My office shelves are lined with favorite books by Tillich, Holmer, Kierkegaard, and Wittgenstein. These books have moved me and consumed me and sometimes saved me. And yet, I maintain an allegiance to one particular book, the Bible, one old and musty book full of strange and wonderful stories from times long before I was born. How is it still possible to lose oneself and find oneself in these stories that glimpse after God?

In this essay, I am arguing that a primary responsibility of preaching is a conscious choice and intentional modeling of the claims of the text on our lives. In order to accomplish this central task, the preacher must develop an awareness about the hermeneutical moves that shape the exegesis of the text and its application and relevance for the listeners.

Preaching in an Information Age

In this data-driven era, it is easy for texts including sermons to become another in a series of information soundbites. The use of technology, especially PowerPoint, tends to exacerbate this tendency. The interest of the preacher is not to provide a set of factual data, but to point to the claims of the gospel upon the lives of listeners. The use of word studies, author information, and historical-critical information regarding the composition of the text is helpful only in so far as it illuminates the world(s) of the text and lays open the similarities and differences between it and the reader. In this process, the preacher cannot lose sight of the fact that the primary purpose of preaching on these texts is to open up and present options about how to live and function in the worlds before us and around us.

It is interesting to note that while in some quarters, criticism of technology in worship continues, preaching ironically may remain on a linear, point-by-point informational basis. Of course there are ways that technology can enhance and undergird the attempt to invite listeners to encounter the claims of the text upon their lives. In this approach, technology serves the purpose of enlarging the imaginative focus of a Scriptural text rather than providing an explanation or a summary of the points of an outline. For example, a wide variety of artistic interpretations of a parable may show the diverse ways in which this text has been pictured by artists throughout history. Similarly, images of the global church can break open the sense of isolation and individualism that are often pervasive in congregations that become overly insular.

Note that the interest here is not specifically on factual or informational claims in a text, but about the way the text opens and invites us into a new world that is larger and different than the enclaves that we create for ourselves. The narrative claim of the text opens our imaginations to search for clues of the presence of the divine. In turn, it provides a pattern for searching for clues in the world(s) around us.

Implications for Preaching

It will be helpful to reflect upon the question of how texts work in order to construct rhetorical strategies for preaching. An awareness of the dynamics of the relationship between reader and text provides clues for how preachers engage the task of encountering the world of the text and interpreting its claim on our lives. Since an encounter with God remains the ultimate *telos* of the gathered assembly, we enter into the world of a text in order to find ourselves before God both in the context of preaching and in the liturgical enactment of Scriptural patterns (sacraments). The narrative world of the text offers us an exploratory adventure into the ecclesial assembly that points to similarities and incongruencies between the worlds in the text and worlds in which we live.

In reflecting upon the ways that texts make claims upon the readers and listeners, I offer a range of options in which the worlds of the text and the reader/listener are held in relationship to one another. These ways are not distinctively separate, but in some sense are part of a spectrum of possibilities in which the reader/hearer discovers ways to live via the text. They are offered as suggestive options to reflect upon the practice of reading and preaching on texts.

The primary differentiation in these approaches is that of the subject-object distance in relationship to the reader and the text. The first two phases retain a certain distance where the discoveries in the world(s) of the text are applied to the world(s) of the readers, while the latter two carry a sense of continuity or discontinuity with the world of the text. In the first of these instances, the reader sees identification with the world(s) of the text and in the second instance, the reader encounters a significant degree of dissonance between the world(s) of the text and the world(s) of the reader.

Following a brief description of these approaches to texts, I offer a theological/philosophical framework for this approach. The framework is intended to be illustrative in providing one way to ground the hermeneutical image in a theoretical model. This approach is descriptive rather than prescriptive, that is, the theological/philosophical model presents a suggestive way (and not a definitive one) of grounding the discussion of the hermeneutical options at work in hearing and responding to texts. Finally, each section concludes with a brief commentary on the homiletical possibilities and trajectories that grow out of this approach.

1. FRAMING—SEEING AS

Reading and interpreting texts is vitally connected to the presentation of particular worldviews. One sees the world in a text in a particular way. This is due both to the inherent worldviews in a text as well as to the worldviews that the readers bring to the text. To some extent, the process of interpretation involves a conversation between the worldviews in the world of the text and the reader/listener's world(s). The narrative dimensions of the text (both the explicit narratives of texts like parables as well as the implicit narratives in the imagined community of the recipients of the epistles) present a particular way of seeing the world and responding to it. The conversation between the worldviews assumes a variety of dimensions. Some are characterized by implied agreement that leads to a shared conclusion. "If a child asked for an egg, what father would give the child a scorpion?"[4] It is assumed that the reader shares the same values and worldview as that in the text. At other times, the conversation expects to create tension. "When they wish to haul you to court to take your shirt, let them have your coat too. If someone asks for your coat, then give them your cloak also."[5] The tension created between the different worldviews allows the text to present an alternative way of seeing the world.

Theological/Philosophical Groundings:

> I should like you to say: "Yes, it's true, that can be imagined, that may even have happened!" But was I trying to draw your attention

4. Luke 11:12 (CEB).
5. Matt 5:40 (CEB).

to the fact that you are able to imagine this? I wanted to put this picture before your eyes, and your *acceptance* of this picture consists in your being inclined to regard a given case differently; that is, to compare it with *this* series of pictures. I have changed your *way of seeing*.[6]

With this brief observation, Ludwig Wittgenstein presents the case for an imaginative way in which language allows us to look at the world in different ways. Language involves a particular point of view that encompasses ways of seeing and being in the world. In this instance, a text presents us with a way to look at the world and with ways to connect and embody the patterns of being in the world. Wittgenstein referred to this in terms of the language games and patterns of language that provide rules, clues, and connections with forms of life (i.e., ways of living in the world). The text becomes a point of orientation that provides its own logic and actions in the context of the world of the text. This alternative world seeks to challenge the readers as well as to present other ways and opportunities of responding to the situations that we face in our own worlds. The text serves as a map of how to orient oneself and move forward in the world of the text. The readers are left to discover and make connections between the world of the text and their own worlds.

Homiletical Implications

The task of the preacher in this instance is to allow the imaginative world of Scripture to present an alternative point of view to those that provide the normative constraints of the listener. Similarly the preacher could point to the language of Scripture and allow it to shape the formation of pictures of the world that would prompt listeners to see it in a different way.

This process of seeing the world in a different way results in different ways of living in the world. Understanding is an act of shared participation in this new way of seeing the world. Thus, the preacher's portrait of a different perspective is at the same time an invitation to a different way of life. Preachers draw out the implications for internal logic of the world in the text and point to connections between the world of the text and the world(s) of the listeners.[7]

6. Wittgenstein, *Zettel*, §461.

7. The use of logic here is not in terms of rationality, but in terms of coherence within a given worldview.

2. MODELING/PATTERNING

Ultimately, the goals of Scripture propose to do more than to present worldviews. Scripture seeks to provide models and patterns for daily life. In this sense, the text itself is a path to conversion in which readers are invited to a dialogue with the world(s) in order to discover models for living in the world of the text that provides patterns for living in the world around them. A typical example of this is that listeners/readers recognize themselves in the contours and characters of the text. Sometimes this may happen in clear and dramatic ways, e.g., the parallels between the parable of the prodigal son and an estranged relationship between father and son. At other times, it may be that the reader/listener develops a sense of comparison between the *Sitz im Leben* of the text of the world and one's own worldview. In some cases, this type of interpretation will follow a kind of archetypal or typological interpretation.

Theological/Philosophical Groundings

Philosopher Paul Ricœur has proposed that we recognize the way in which texts offer the readers worlds that are constructed by language and symbol that express particular ontological understandings with teleological aims. Language strives to point beyond itself in order to disclose reality.

> Language is that through which, by means of which, we express ourselves and express things. To speak is the act by which the speaker overcomes the closure of the universe of signs, in the intention of saying something about something to someone; to speak is the act by which language moves beyond itself as sign toward its opposite. Language seeks to disappear; it seeks to die as an object.[8]

The shift from orality to textuality brings with it the possibility of a new world that is created which serves as a bridge between events behind the text and events in the reader's world. By opening up the language of the text, the listener/reader is placed in a position to encounter a shared world between that of the text and his/her own world.

---

8. Ricœur, *Philosophy of Paul Ricœur,* 112.

Homiletical Implications

In this instance, the task of the preacher is to allow the symbolic language of the world of the text to place its claims on the world(s) of the hearers. Symbols act as signs or pointers to something that is beyond the text. The act of interpreting symbols includes a form of existential commitment to the world of the text. The preacher's own commitment to these deep truths points to a way of understanding that is not behind the symbols, but shows a way of thinking and living according to the symbols.

Particular care should be taken not to substitute symbolic layers that may disrupt the process of understanding. Preachers have a responsibility to avoid exchanging one world of meaning for a completely different one. For example, the use of popular imagery can substitute a different world than the one in the text. Nowhere is this more clear than ill-fated attempts to use Easter bunnies as examples for the resurrection in Easter sermons. Here the dramatic claims of the theological images in a text are substituted by a cultural cliché that lacks the ability to point to deeper ways of responding to the claims of the text on our lives.

3. IDENTIFICATION: CULTIVATING A STRONG SENSE OF CONNECTION WITH THE TEXT

In this approach, even more than the recognition of parallels between world of text and world of listener, the listener is taken deep into the text in order to discover meaning and value. One's own world is overwhelmed by the world that one discovers in the text. It is as if one has entered a completely different world in which the rules of conduct must be discovered. The compelling nature of this world pulls the hearer into it in order that one may discover meaning in it. The meaning resides not in reflections upon the relationship between the reader and the text, but in the engagement within the world of the text. It is only later that the reader will seek to apply the textual interfaces to the situations in her own world(s).

Theological/Philosophical Groundings

In his work on hermeneutics, Hans Frei called for a return to a realistic reading of biblical narratives. His approach fosters an appreciation for biblical narrative as that which shapes and alters reality. The world of the story is the decisive world and determines the reader's world. Realistic narrative presents this "real world" to its readers. This reading of the text

> renders for us by way of story a common world of discourse, the world we need to understand the story—the same kind of world as ours, the world in which persons and circumstances shape each other . . . In that way, the gospel story and we ourselves inhabit the same kind of world.[9]

Following clues from Karl Barth's theology, Frei describes the ways in which the world of the text provides a coherent pattern that seeks to be a determinative interpretive model for providing readers with ways to live in their world. The biblical narrative establishes the perspective that interprets the hearer/reader's world.

> It is the effective rendering of God and his [God's] real world to the reader by way of the text's appropriate depiction of the intercourse of that God and of that world, engaging the reader's mind, heart, and activity.[10]

The text looms as *a priori* over the lives of the reader. Engagement with and immersion into the world of the text becomes the source of coherence for the reader to understand correctly the world(s) around them.

Homiletical Implications

The primary task of preaching in this instance is an invitation into the world of the text. The sermon seeks to overlay the narrative of the text onto the narratives of our lives. In that sense, the world of the text sets out to overwhelm the world of the listener so that it provides the dominant framework for understanding meaning. In reflecting on the application of Frei's work for homileticians, Chuck Campbell concludes that: "With respect to sermon form, Frei himself seemed most concerned to move from biblical text to contemporary situation, rather than 'inductively' from human experience to the text."[11]

I believe that much African-American preaching has skillfully followed this model in the sustained attention to the parallels between the Hebrew slaves in Egypt and the plight of African Americans. In these

9. Frei, "Theology and the Interpretation of Narrative," 27.

10. Frei, *Eclipse of Biblical Narrative*, 25.

11. Campbell, *Preaching Jesus*, 203.

sermons, the responses of the biblical figures provide clues and patterns for ways that the listeners can respond to the experiences of captivity and slavery in their own lives.

4. TEXT AS COUNTERPOINT

In this regard, the world of the text stands over and against our worlds. The task here is not so much with identification within the world of text as with a recognition of dissonance that prompts listeners to seek a source of transformation with their worlds(s). The strangeness of the textual world creates a sense of tension in which one hopes that the world around oneself can more closely mirror the relationships and actions within the world of the text.

Theological/Philosophical Groundings: In *Concluding Unscientific Postscript to Philosophical Fragments*

Søren Kierkegaard describes the difficulties of becoming a Christian (as opposed to accepting the culture of Christendom). He concludes that, "One should not chaffer, should not want to alter Christianity, should not overdo the thing by putting up resistance at the wrong place, but should simply take care that it remains what it was, to the Jews, a stumbling block and to the Greeks foolishness."[12]

Homiletical implications:

The preacher has to paint the contrast between the readers' worlds and the world of the text. In doing so, the preacher seeks to prod and prompt a sense of longing for this other world. Here the goal of preaching is for the demands of this other world to be clear while pointing to the sense of longing in the listener to accept and believe the absolute paradox. In a sermon on the transfiguration, John Fry described the unusual qualities of the description in the text that are set over against the expectations of the disciples and the listeners. In the end, Fry concludes with a testimony to the dramatic struggle of yielding to this light in his own life and yet the difficulty of giving one's life over to that which is strange and different.[13]

12. Kierkegaard, *Concluding Unscientific Postscript*, 535.
13. John R. Fry, Unpublished sermon, February 1996.

CONCLUSION

The preacher carries a responsibility for developing a conscious sense about how to make sound and appropriate hermeneutical choices given both the nature of a particular biblical text and the realities of a local context. It is the one who proclaims, who seeks to show ways in which the text and context intersect in order that the power of the Word by the working of the Spirit may fully engage, support, disrupt, and confront the hearers. In this process, the preacher seeks to model ways that others can develop consciousness and responsibility for the theological and hermeneutical options for encountering and presenting the Word and the claims of the text on our lives.

In the final analysis, a renewed emphasis on the role of Scripture and preaching provides a primary way of encouraging worshipers to experience ways that a biblical text makes claims on their lives. This approach to preaching supports the broad goals of building biblical literacy and encouraging spiritual growth by showing ways in which encounters with biblical texts mark and shape the lives of Christians.

5

Preaching as Cultivating
a Sacramental Imagination

A PRIMARY GOAL OF preaching is to show ways that Scripture addresses our lives by opening up new ways for hearers to encounter and live the claims of the gospel. The sermon models ways in which listeners can engage with the text. The meaning of the sermon also grows out of its context in the liturgy. Postmodern interpreters have shown ways that listeners create meaning by drawing connections between events. In the context of worship, participants will make connections between the reading of biblical texts and the actions of worship. This is not only a case of individuals making particular connections, but is also embedded into the fabric of the liturgy. For example, the selection of texts for the common lectionary anticipates that the biblical texts are accompanied by the celebration of communion. Thus, the language of eating and drinking often prefigures the act of receiving the bread and cup. Similarly, on holy days where baptisms are anticipated (for example on the Baptism of the Lord or at the Easter Vigil), the readings often include references to water and healing that anticipate the actions of the assembly around the baptismal font.

Preachers who approach the task with an awareness of these multiple dimensions will be better able to anticipate connections that worshipers will make between the reading of biblical texts and the liturgical actions of the assembly. Liturgical preaching is a particular type of proclamation in the way that it deliberately seeks to engage the entire liturgical setting in order to encourage the assembly to change our perspectives on the way that we hear Scripture and the way that we see the world around us. Like other forms of preaching, liturgical preaching is grounded in Scripture but extends its scope to engage with the sacraments and the broader liturgical setting. In this chapter, I will offer an overview of what key characteristics and approaches that liturgical preaching uses in order to persuade listeners to see ourselves and the world around us from a new perspective. Here, I am drawing on the philosophical work of Ludwig Wittgenstein who described the ways in which the images that we create open up new ways of seeing ourselves and the world around us.

> Well, I should like you to say: "Yes, it's true, you can imagine that too, that might happen too!"—But was I trying to draw someone's attention to the fact that he is capable of imaging that?—I wanted to put that picture before him, and his *acceptance* of the picture consists in his now being inclined to regard a given case differently: that is to compare with *this* rather than *that* set of pictures. I have changed his *way of looking at things*.[1]

From this perspective, preaching holds the possibility of supporting the work of transformation as it shows ways that texts and our surrounding actions prompt us to see ourselves in new ways. We will examine four interrelated elements: Scripture, sacraments, space, and assembly to look for clues about how these pieces may fit together in holistic ways.

SCRIPTURE

Sermons are grounded in and engage with Scripture as the Word is read and proclaimed. While this sounds straightforward, it remains an elusive art. In what ways does preaching mine the riches of Scripture in order that the hearers may respond to the claims of the gospel on our lives? Modern biblical scholarship provides a set of rigorous approaches in order that the meaning(s) of a text can be properly identified. In seminaries today, strict critical-exegetical skills continue to be taught in order that the reader/interpreter of Scripture can identify the "proper understanding" of a biblical text. In this process, the emphasis remains closely identified with the historical setting of the text and author. While I do not want to diminish the significant insights that biblical scholarship continues to provide readers

1. Wittgenstein, *Philosophical Investigations*, PI 144, p. 57e. For more on Wittgenstein's applicability to liturgical theology, see my book *Doxology and Theology*.

of Scripture, it is also important to make room for other ways of reading Scripture that the church has valued in its history.

Liturgical preaching draws on the broad history of interpretation of Scripture. In the third century CE, Origen of Alexandria outlined an approach to interpreting Scripture that began with a literal/historical approach before moving on to higher modes of understanding of texts that included the moral and spiritual sense of the text. The spiritual sense of a text often was based on allegorical and typological interpretations. In the history of interpreting biblical texts, tension grew over abuses of the allegorical method of interpretation. Eventually, reformers like Luther and Calvin advocated for the study of texts in order to determine the plain sense (perspicuity—in Luther's case) or for the beginning of a more critical examination of the text. These approaches to Scripture were efforts to encourage biblical literacy. Ironically, the development of scientific approaches to interpretation of Scripture and the advent of specialization of scholarship worked in some ways against the basic goal of promoting engagement with the text. More and more, the interpretation of biblical texts was left in the hands of biblical scholars to identify the meaning(s) of a particular text. Liturgical preaching is that which seeks to use the insights of biblical scholars, but recognizes that scholarship (no matter how careful and well-crafted) will not be able to fix a meaning(s) to the text. Instead, liturgical preaching sees the art of proclamation as an opportunity to point the listeners into the mysterious world of the text.

In a stunning critique of the arrogance of biblical scholars who believe that they alone can identify the proper meaning of a text, literary scholar Frank Kermode points to the ineffability of textual worlds.

> Much of what I have said will be disallowed by defenders of a hermeneutics more conservative than mine, and doubtless with scorn, by a flourishing radical party, which would not admit that its investigations are properly to be called hermeneutic, and which despises the very word "interpretation." Yet we are all, on a broad enough view, concerned with the same problem. Some suppose that it is right to inquire strictly into the question of what the text originally meant. Others wish to discover what it originally means, a more charismatic quest . . . Yet all practice divination, however intermittently, erroneously, dishonestly, or disappointedly.[2]

2. Kermode, *Genesis of Secrecy*, 125–26.

The liturgical preacher understands that her role is not to find the meaning(s) of a text. Instead, preaching becomes an act of the imagination that leads to the possible encounter with the Mystery in the text.

> We are most unwilling to accept mystery, what cannot be reduced to other and more intelligible forms. Yet that is what we find here: something irreducible, therefore perpetually to be interpreted; not secrets to be found out one by one, but Secrecy.[3]

This imaginative engagement with the world(s) of the text is the scope of liturgical preaching, which seeks to present Secrecy to the hearers. To this end, liturgical preaching makes use of the resources of the liturgy in order to open the text in new ways and to present new possibilities.

The widespread acceptance of the Revised Common Lectionary has provided a major impetus by selecting texts that often carry sacramental associations. As we have previously noted, the lectionary was developed specifically for services of Word and Table, and therefore it is not surprising that food images are replete throughout the texts. Similarly, water images are common throughout the three year cycle. Congregations that adopted the lectionary readings (even partially) encountered sacramental images (often subliminally) week after week. In many of these congregations, parishioners listened to texts replete with feeding images while looking across an empty communion table. Similarly, texts full of water and washing images were read in congregations where the baptismal font was empty and/or pushed to the side. In these instances, the power of the Word alone began to prompt both preacher and listener to encounter these texts in new ways. Note how the images of water, food, and drink in the lectionary serve as sacramental signs that point to both the presence and absence of the celebration of the sacraments in the life of a congregation. The lectionary prepared the way for congregations to begin a time of sacramental renewal. This period of renewal has been accompanied and supported by the recovery of preaching that engages the sacraments and points steadily to connections between Word and Sacrament.

SACRAMENTS

Since biblical texts are filled with sacramental images, liturgical preaching engages the sacraments as places of encounter. This approach to preaching

3. Kermode, *Genesis of Secrecy*, 143.

requires cultivating a sacramental imagination. David Power describes this process:

> To open the sacramental imagination, whether to other cultures or to the post[-]modern, communities have to learn by experience to forego that kind of representational imagery which tries to bring the past or the divine into immediate presence, by the power of institution, the power of ritual imitation or the power of conceptual thought and locution.[4]

The development of a sacramental imagination on behalf of liturgical preaching moves actively beyond the reading of Scripture from the primary perspective of the historical-critical method. To accomplish this goal, preachers develop the skill of recognizing associations between the reading of the text and the place of the sacraments in the life of our communities of faith.

For several semesters, I gave students in my classes on sacraments the assignment of writing a journal on sacramental images in the daily lectionary. The result of this exercise followed a normative pattern. During the first month, the majority of students are unable and/or unwilling to make associations between Scripture readings and the sacraments. The tyranny of the historical-critical method dominates their imaginations. For example, when reflecting on the Exodus narrative of the Hebrew children crossing the Red Sea, students noted that while the text includes references to water and deliverance to new life, it would be inappropriate to read Christian themes into this Hebrew Scripture. Over the course of the semester, students gradually grew into new ways of associating the images in Scripture with the sacraments. This process of cultivating a sacramental imagination lies at the center of liturgical preaching. The preacher's own commitment to the sacramental life of the church nurtures and supports imaginative ways of reading Scripture in which the sacraments serve as primary focal points for the community's life together. In this sense, liturgical preaching is the deliberative art of public reflection that provides patterns for the congregation's own reading of Scripture.

In a survey done by the research office in the Presbyterian Church (U.S.A.), pastors and members were asked to indicate the degree of relevance between selected Bible passages and the Lord's Supper. Predictably, at the top of the list were two texts often associated with Jesus' Last Supper: Luke 22 ("Do this in remembrance of me") and 1 Corinthians 11 ("As

4. Power, *Sacrament*, 173.

often as you eat this bread").[5] Even this is suggestive of the highly truncated form of imagination that dominates many of our congregations' approach towards communion. What is even more shocking is that texts with primary eucharistic imagery were largely ignored and overlooked. The Acts 2 narrative of the life of the early church's practice of breaking bread with glad and generous hearts was deemed very significant or significant to the Lord's Supper by less than one third of the members of the congregations (32 percent) and just over one half of the pastors (54 percent). Luke 24 (the road to Emmaus) was rated as very significant or significant by similar amounts of members (31 percent) and more pastors (66 percent).[6] Jesus' resurrection meal with the disciples (John 21) was not even included on the list of texts. Similarly shocking results are associated with questions about baptism where wide majorities of the members and pastors (nearly three-fourths) identified Jesus welcoming the little children in Matthew 19 as very significant or significant presumably because of its historical/ theological use as a proof text for infant baptism. Yet, texts with associative connections to baptism like John 4 (the woman at the well) were not even part of the survey.[7]

In the face of these strict limitations on our imaginations, liturgical preaching seeks to prompt the practice of sacramental readings of texts and the world around us. It eschews the claim to primacy of the cognitive and rational explanations and invites the listeners to reflect on the possibility of encountering the Divine in and through these ordinary things around which we gather: this book, this water, this bread and wine. In place of logical forms of articulation about the proper meaning of a text in light of its historical background, liturgical preaching makes room and invites the listeners to develop and exercise imaginative associations in light of this text. In this regard, I am not arguing for the abandonment of theological arguments and careful exegesis of Scripture. Instead, I am urging that these acts be accompanied by reflections on the ways in which biblical texts connect to the sacramental practices that sustain the lives of our communities.

5. Research Services, "Sacraments."
6. Research Services, "Sacraments."
7. Research Services, "Sacraments."

ASSEMBLY

Liturgical preaching understands its role as that which encourages and supports the assembly's active participation in the imaginative acts of connecting the liturgy with daily life. Rather than providing the congregation with prescriptive solutions or required beliefs, liturgical preaching, in this sense, fosters an associative rendering of Word and Sacrament with the day-to-day lives of congregational members. This approach to preaching is suggestive in nature in the way that it opens up and offers interpretive options for linking Word, Sacrament, and World.

Mystagogical sermons that reflect on shared experiences provide one prominent way of examining our experiences (in this sense often sacramental) in light of texts and reflecting on their intersections and connections. For example, sermons that reflect on the experience of baptism at the Easter Vigil provide the broader congregation with an interpretive lens for ways to encounter a biblical text and participate in shared reflection whether or not members of the congregation actually attended this service. In this way, liturgical preaching invites the congregation into an imagined world in which all are welcome to this anamnestic practice of being re-membered into the life of Christ. By picturing shared events, the primacy of the community's life together is upheld and interpreted. A related approach is when the preacher renders an interpretive narrative of the events of his own life in light of the claims of Scripture, thus modeling for the community ways to read and interpret our own lives in light of Scripture. Preaching becomes a way of encouraging listeners to look for the signs of God's presence in our lives, a form of holy patterning about the possibility of seeing Mystery in the ordinariness of our daily lives. Here, liturgical preaching understands its actions as a starting place rather than as an end in itself. This form of proclamation offers patterns rather than theological diagnosis or prescriptive solutions. The assembly is welcomed into the discourse as a way of encouraging reflection by the congregation as they seek to discern the presence of the Mystery in their own lives and in our lives together.

SPACE

Liturgical preaching is not content to reside within the safe confines of a pulpit or of ecclesial space. Instead, it recognizes the gathering space as a starting place for reclaiming the assembly's full participation in the incarnational work of the gospel in the world. As Western culture continues the process of throwing off the cloak of Christendom, many of our congregations are facing the growing awareness of life on the margins of society. It is increasingly difficult to assume that the church is near the center of cultural power. Thus the church finds itself trapped between nostalgia for the ways things used to be and the temptation of isolating ourselves from the world around us. It is at this very point that liturgical preaching has the possibility of pointing us in a new direction. Rather than retreat from the world to the splendid isolation of our sanctuaries, liturgical preaching places us in the world in order that we may encounter the risen Christ beyond the walls of our church buildings. By teaching us to read and hear texts in new ways, by cultivating a sacramental imagination, by stressing the primary role of community in an age of individualism and privatism, liturgical preaching engages in the practice of creating associations between the liturgy, the assembly, and the world around us.

I have noticed a common use of liturgical language that urges us to go forth from the liturgy into the world. Implied in this language is an assumption that the church is somehow a place separate from the world: a place that we retreat from the world and a place to which we return. The church has often reinforced such an understanding by framing the sacraments primarily in terms of spirituality. Liturgical preaching that emphasizes the connection of biblical texts, with the ordinary things of the sacraments and the ordinary things of our lives has the possibility of providing an important corrective to our speech. Here the church is envisioned not as a place apart from the world around us, a place where we go for correction and instruction about how to survive out there in the world. Rather, the church as the body of Christ serves as an incarnational sign *in* the world. This approach to preaching takes its cue from the great twentieth-century German theologian Dietrich Bonhoeffer, who summed it up: "the primary reason for the church is to provide physical space for the body of Christ in the world."[8] Liturgical preaching underscores the physicality of our bodies, of this place, of these things around which we gather in the hope and possibility that, like the disciples on the road to Emmaus, our eyes might be opened in the breaking of the bread. Liturgy as an embodied act demonstrates ways

8. Bonhoeffer, *Ethics*. See also, Bonhoeffer, *Discipleship*, 225, n. 2 where Bonhoeffer puts this slightly differently in his note to seminarians about upcoming lectures on the New Testament: "The present situation in church and theology can be summed up in the following question: Does the church take up a space in the world, and if so, what kind of space is it?"

in which our bodies relate to one another and to the world around us. These physical acts are performative responses that engage our bodies and map out ways that we incarnate the gospel. Cláudio Carvalhaes pictures this in his essay, "'Gimme de kneebone bent': Liturgics, Dance, Resistance and a Hermeneutics of the Knees":

> The knees have always been a dangerous element in the Christian faith. In spite of the doctrine of the incarnation, God's *excessive knee movement* in Christ, the Christian body in general remained, a frightened space where things can easily get out of control.[9]

Liturgical preaching has the possibility of reclaiming our bodies as a primary locus of God's ongoing act of creation where our connection to one another and our connection to the earth and to all of God's good creation are signs of faithful discipleship. The embodied preacher raises her voice and points to these things around which our bodies gather in order to prompt our imaginations to see the Spirit at work in our lives. This radical act of reclaiming space for our bodies in worship leads Carvalhaes to conclude:

> A feminist approach to the knees is just the first stop on this road of hermeneutics of the body, an approach that should be always corrected by other knee movements and thoughts. Then we should take on Shakira's suggestions and de-construct the hips, then the hands, the feet, the hair, the belly, the eyes, the mouth, the vagina, the neck, the penis, the skin and so on. Paraphrasing Derrida, I would say that the constancy of God in my life is called by other movements of the body.[10]

Making space for our bodies to respond to Christ's invitation to follow him lies at the heart of liturgical preaching. This disruptive process invites us out of the passive posture of our pews and into a full-bodied response to the Word who was made flesh and dwelt among us. In these incarnational movements, liturgical preaching brings together text, sacraments, assembly, and space in order that we may see and encounter the One who shows us the way, truth, and life.

---

9. Carvalhaes, "'Gimme de Kneebone Bent,'" 2.
10. Carvalhaes, "'Gimme de Kneebone Bent,'" 16.

CONCLUSION

In the end, through the work of the Holy Spirit, the goal of all preaching is transformation. Namely that through an encounter with this text, in this place, with these people, we may discover a new way to look at ourselves and the world around us differently. This conversion process is the disruptive possibility of encountering grace that will change our vision. Liturgical preaching provides a particular set of lenses that foster the development of this new sight. Years ago, I read a psychological study of an experiment where subjects were given a set of glasses that caused them to see the world upside down.[11] As a part of the study, the subjects were required to wear the glasses every day for a period of one week. In the initial days, the subjects reported the expected difficulties of dislocation walking into objects. However in a relatively short period of time, the subjects had adjusted to this new way of seeing the world. They had learned to navigate according to this new way of seeing. At the end of the study, when they took off the glasses, they experienced similar disorientation and needed time in order to re-adapt to another way of seeing the world around them. Or as Wittgenstein described:

> I wanted to put this picture before your eyes, and your *acceptance* of this picture consists in your being inclined to regard a given case differently; that is, to compare it with *this* series of pictures. I have changed your *way of seeing.*[12]

Liturgical preaching presents the claims of Scripture on our lives in the context of the worshiping assembly in order that we may experience a new way of seeing and respond to the call to discipleship. Liturgical preaching seeks to change the ways we see, hear, and live out the claims of the gospel on our lives.

---

11. Pendergrast, *Mirror, Mirror*, 213.
12. Wittgenstein, *Zettel*, Z461, p. 82e.

6

Sacramental Models for Daily Life

THROUGHOUT THE HISTORY OF the church, there have been significant debates over different theological perspectives on Christ's presence at the table. It is not the purpose of this chapter to plow through these often obscure points of contention one more time. Instead, our attention is focused on the role and purpose of Jesus as model and focal point of the communion prayer. In framing the discussion in these terms, we hope to avoid the deep level of debates in pursuit of an alternative route into the purpose of eucharistic prayer and into the role of sacraments as models for our daily lives.[1] While the areas of historical conflict cannot be avoided altogether, a brief discussion of terms and distinctions between different Christian traditions will lead to a more fulsome exploration of the christological center of communion prayer.

In late medieval times, the conversations on this topic led to historic divisions in the church. At the center of the Reformation debate was a re-examination of sacrificial notions in the Mass. In Geneva, John Calvin re-oriented communion practices by moving the altar into the congregation and referring to it as a table. The significance of this was to distance the worship actions from any associations with the mass as a re-sacrifice of Christ. In Zurich, Ulrich Zwingli went even further by sending the elements into

1. This essay is adapted from my book *Leading from the Table*. I first began using the language of Sacramental Ethics in 2004 with encouragement and support from Joe Small. The language seeks to highlight the need to draw out the implications of celebrating the sacraments and our daily lives. For further discussion, see my "Doing Justice with a Sacramental Heart," 3–10 and "Sacramental Ethics: Making Public Worship Public," 56–61.

the congregation in order that worshipers would not continue to approach the altar as they did in the mass.

It is important to note that these debates often included crass mischaracterizations of the opponent's position. On the one hand, Protestants' inflammatory attacks on the graphic re-sacrificing of Christ by Roman Catholic priests failed to recognize a more nuanced view held by many within the Catholic Church. Likewise, Roman Catholics often had difficulty accepting more qualified notions of the events taking place at the table. Lost in this struggle was the large area of agreement between many of the participants that the communion prayer, with its focus on thanksgiving, was grounded in the story of Jesus Christ.

CENTERING ON CHRIST

There is growing awareness among liturgical scholars that the entirety of the Gospels provides insight into the church's development of sacramental practices. Thus, meals during Jesus' public ministry and post-resurrection meals offer significant insights and commentary on ways for us to gather to break bread and share the cup in thanksgiving as we remember Jesus Christ.[2] Focusing the conversation around the centrality of Christ in our communion practices allows us to emphasize the primary area of agreements between denominations rather than replay theological debates.

In the very structure of the communion prayer itself, Jesus Christ is central. After the recognition of creation as expressive of God's glory and the remembrance of God's faithfulness in sending prophets to call God's people back to the covenant, the prayer turns to Jesus. In the fullness of time is language that parallels the gospel understandings of a *kairos* moment. Such a time speaks less of simple chronology than it does about when the time is right. At the proper time or in just the right moment, Jesus comes to present God's redemptive work in our world.

This central part of the shape of the prayer at table follows the outline of Jesus' birth, ministry, death, and resurrection. As a summary of Jesus' life, the prayer becomes a form of gospel proclamation in its own right. As proclamation, it is important for the prayer to present a brief portrait of

2. Roman Catholic biblical scholars like Raymond Brown have been particularly helpful in identifying sacramental images throughout the Gospels. For example, note Brown's frequent connections to the sacraments in his commentary on the Gospel of John.

Jesus' life. Rather than simply rush to the cross and present a theological interpretation of atonement,[3] prayers from the table point to the broader contours of Jesus' life. Born of Mary, Jesus lives as God's grace among us. While theologians often speak of the integral connection between baptism and communion (communion as the repeatable part of baptism), it seems odd that Jesus' baptism is rarely mentioned in communion prayers. One exception is the Communion prayer for the Sunday of the Baptism of the Lord. Here, the prayer includes these words:

> Baptized in Jordan's waters,
> Jesus took his place with sinners
> and your voice proclaimed him your beloved.[4]

This language not only reinforces basic baptismal imagery, but provides a vision of Jesus' solidarity with all who come in response to God's invitation. The wording also provides a basis for a further exploration of the church's declaration that in baptism, all of us are declared beloved children of God. In this sense, the portrait of solidarity shows Jesus' identification with us as sinners in his baptism and our identification with Christ in God's acceptance of us as sons and daughters in our baptism.

As part of the retelling of the life of Jesus, prayers that include Jesus' baptism as a defining moment in his vocational identity at the onset of his public ministry provide a foundation for us to discover this integral connection in our own calling as Christians. As Jesus' baptism led to engagement in public ministry, so too do our own baptisms mark the beginning of discernment about our gifts and calling as disciples of Jesus Christ.[5]

Following Jesus' birth and baptism, the prayer at the table turns to basic themes and acts that mark his public ministry. His teaching and healing made God's reign visible. In solidarity with the poor, he lived a simple life. He welcomed strangers and broke bread with sinners and outcasts. He proclaimed the good news of the kingdom of God to all people. When a brief outline of Jesus' life is included, the prayer offers a more holistic vision that serves as a primary example of ways we can follow in Christ's footsteps.

3. For a helpful discussion of the variety of biblical and theological models of atonement, see Fiddes, *Past Event and Present Salvation*.

4. Presbyterian Church (U.S.A.)., *Book of Common Worship*, 201.

5. The catechumenate as a model of baptismal preparation is particularly helpful with its emphasis on a mystagogical understanding of the experience of baptism that includes an exploration of the gifts and opportunities for service for those who have recently been baptized.

Even the language of the Lord's table and the Lord's Supper seeks to point to Christ as the primary foundation for gathering at the table. Thus, it is important for communion prayers to provide a broad sketch that includes Jesus' birth, baptism, public ministry of healing, teaching, welcoming, and judging. The public ministry and confrontation with religious and political powers is what prompts the events that lead to Jesus' death in Jerusalem. Communion prayers should provide a context for the cross as a way of speaking of the past and as a way to point to the need for Christians to live and speak of the cost of discipleship today.

LIFE AND DEATH AT THE CROSSROADS

What is the purpose of the description of Jesus in the communion prayer? There is a decided lack of agreement between—and even within—denominations on this basic question. In some prayers, the language about Jesus is framed in such a way as to present a theological interpretation that focuses on the cross as a source of salvation. Other prayers (and particularly some of the more recent ones) use broader language to present a more holistic presentation of Jesus' life, ministry, death, and resurrection. The purpose in these prayers is not to diminish the place of the cross in any way. Among all Christians, the cross stands as *the* basic symbol of God's presence in the midst of human pain and suffering. All faithful accounts of the Jesus narrative include the suffering endured by Jesus on the cross. However, it is worth asking whether or not communion prayers that focus on a particular interpretation of the doctrine of atonement actually do justice to the portrait of Jesus presented in the Gospels.

When the prayer provides a summary of the life of Jesus then it serves as a proclamation of the gospel for the entire assembly. It also foreshadows and models a basic outline of Christian life. Christian commitment to solidarity with the poor, feeding the hungry, clothing the naked, visiting the imprisoned, and tending to the sick and neglected can discover a foundation when leaders offer prayers that point to these basic components of Jesus' ministry and our Christian callings.

The role of the communion prayer must, however, point to the reality of sacrifice that is a part of this vision of Christian discipleship. In this sense, nearly all forms of communion prayer point to the cross as evidence for the price of conflict between Jesus and the established religious and political powers. The vision of God's reign that welcomes all people comes into sharp conflict with authorities in Jerusalem and that leads to Jesus' suffering and death. Here again the prayer serves as a model and also as a warning about the high cost of discipleship for those who follow in Jesus' steps.

Communion prayers that present the gospel in brief offer a testimony that is grounded in Jesus' faithful witness. This testimony serves as a road map to those who wish to follow Christ's example. The Eucharistic Prayer is a presentation of the life of Jesus that seeks to lay an imprint of service and sacrifice alongside our lives. Christ's life serves as an icon/image for shaping our lives. The importance of this is in the portrait of Jesus that is presented in the communion prayer. If the prayer only recounts the sacrificial death of Jesus, then we are left with virtually no pattern for our own lives. Since it is unlikely that we will be persecuted, let alone martyred for our faith, solely focusing on the cross in this section of the communion prayers fails to provide us with a template for how to live our lives. Thus, when the primary image is of Jesus' sacrificial death, we are separated from the incarnation rather than drawn into it. Communion prayers that present a wider collage of Jesus' life have an opportunity to guide us in distinctive ways of living as followers of Jesus Christ.

For example, to include a mention of Jesus' care for the poor is to insert and reassert the basic biblical claim that God has a particular interest in the plight of the poor. The prayer invites us to take on this claim as we live in light of the Jesus story. To speak of Jesus' acts of healing and exorcism are to call those who come to the table to tend to the needs of the sick and to fight the forces of evil and oppression in our society. To recall that Jesus ate with sinners and outcasts is to challenge us to share our food with those we sometimes judge or ignore. It is in this broader sketch of Jesus' life that the power of the cross finds its place. In the communion prayer, the cross and Jesus' suffering serve as a warning that there is a cost of faithful discipleship. Similar to Jesus' words to his first disciples about the high price of following him, the communion prayer reminds us that while God's grace is freely offered, lives of service will require us to make sacrifices. In the midst of this word of warning, the communion prayer also offers a word of hope. To speak of the resurrection is to point to our assurance that God will continue to breathe new life into our world, our communities, and ourselves. In the words of St. Paul, as we die to the self, God brings us new life. Resurrection is not simply a theological event attached to Jesus' life, it is God's promise to all believers that in the midst of death, we will receive new life.

OBLATION AND OBLIGATION

Our conversation leads to a broader examination of the role of sacrifice and offering in the communion prayer. To put the issue in its basic form: What is being offered at the communion table? Church traditions have gone in drastically different ways in answer to this question. There is a wide spectrum of positions on the nature of sacrifice in the communion meal. Some have argued that communion is the representation of the physical body of Christ while others have suggested that the primary role is to remind us of the sacrifice Jesus made long ago. One option that has been suggested is to view the congregation's praise and thanksgiving as an offering and sacrifice.[6] The strength of this perspective is that it builds on notions of the assembly's active participation in the prayer. While there are positive elements of this understanding, it fails to demonstrate how the assembly's prayer of thanksgiving is actually offering a sacrifice.[7]

I wish to avoid much of the discussion that has historically divided the church and instead focus on a basic, biblical claim that can unite us as we gather at the table. In Romans 12:1, the Apostle Paul invites us to present *ourselves* as a living sacrifice. "I appeal to you therefore, brothers and sisters, by the mercies of God, to present your bodies as a living sacrifice, holy and acceptable to God, which is your spiritual [reasonable] worship." Instead of engaging in endless debate about theological interpretations of the eucharistic prayer, Paul is inviting us to understand ourselves as the offering that is presented to God. Our act of worship is to come to the table to receive God's grace and blessings in order for our lives to take on the shape of Christ's life in the world. We present ourselves as a living sacrifice so that our work is no longer self-serving, but is done in service of God's redemptive presence in the world. Coming to the table is part of the transformation of our lives from self-concern and consumption to becoming the body of Christ in and for the world around us.

Leading from the table is a way of extending an altar call to the entire congregation to invite all to lives of discipleship. This practice is an ongoing

---

6. Ron Byars offers this suggestion in *Lift Your Hearts on High*, 29. He offers this perspective as a sharp contrast to the medieval understanding of the Mass as Christ's sacrifice.

7. It is worth noting that this perspective grew out of the Reformed tradition where the communion prayer has often carried a penitential nature. If we are seeking to recover the practice of a joyful feast, it is difficult for me to see how this is a sacrificial act on the part of the congregation.

and gradual transformation of our lives into the life of Christ. Paul speaks of this process as part of a continual struggle to allow God to reshape his life into a model of Christ's life. For Paul, the language of dying to self is grounded in the imagery of baptism where the old self is buried and we put on Christ. "So if anyone is in Christ, there is a new creation; everything old has passed away; see everything has become new" (2 Cor 5:17). While in some places Paul writes that this is accomplished in baptism, at other times he talks about the ongoing struggle to live according to the spirit rather than the flesh. In Galatians 5, Paul speaks about cultivating the fruits of the Spirit as signs of the new life that we have in Christ.

Communion as an ongoing reaffirmation of our baptism is a primary way of growing into this new life. At the table, we hear and see again the shape of Christ's life as a shape for our own lives.[8] In response to the invitation, we come to offer our lives in thanksgiving and service for God's grace. The prayer at the table presents a claim upon our lives that points to ways of living the life of Christ in our world. At the table, nourishment is offered by the Spirit through the presence of Christ in the elements and in one another. The table provides both the deep soil that allows the roots of our Christian life to grow as well as the nourishment that will enable us to blossom and produce fruits of Christian living.

PUTTING IT INTO PRACTICE

So what difference does this form of communion prayer make? Prayers that follow the narrative of Jesus' life as an outline for Christian discipleship will take distinctive forms within individual communities. Authentic Christian faith is contextual. As the shape of Jesus' life is overlaid upon the contours of our own lives, we find our unique calling and witness. Thus, I am not suggesting a single, prescriptive portrait of the Christian life. Instead, I want to point to unique responses that take on characteristics of the Jesus narrative within local communities. Below are several vignettes that show the significance of the eucharistic prayer in forming communities that reflect Jesus' commitments and practices.

> *In downtown Tacoma, Nativity House provided a safe place for homeless people to eat and spend the day while the shelters were closed. Each week members of the staff joined with street people for a brief worship service with communion. A group of homeless people*

8. Following Augustine, Calvin often referred to the sacraments as "visible words."

gathered in a small make-shift chapel. Chronic issues of addiction and mental illness beset many of the participants. Even the act of reading Scripture together took on interesting and unusual dimensions as one quickly learned that volunteer readers were likely to add their own commentary to the reading of the passage. On a Friday morning, I arrived to lead the service. At the time of communion, I offered a brief eucharistic prayer that highlighted Jesus' commitment to serving the poor and alienated. As I began serving the elements of bread and juice to those in the room, I found my own life under conviction for the ways that I often ignored the plight of the homeless in my own community. It was clear to me that day that Jesus would have spent much more time in places like this than in many of the places where I did much of my work.

At a worship service on the twentieth anniversary of the killing of Oscar Romero, a broad ecumenical group listened to the testimony of his life and teachings. The service included readings from Romero's sermons and teaching on the importance of the church's solidarity with the poor. The communion liturgy was framed by Romero's call to transform our communities of faith into centers that work for justice. "The church would betray its own love for God and its fidelity to the gospel if it stopped being . . . a defender of the rights of the poor . . . a humanizer of every legitimate struggle to achieve a more just society . . . that prepares the way for the true reign of God in history."[9] Following communion, a group of Native Americans handed out Sacagawea dollar coins to all those who were present as a gift in memory of Romero's sacrifice. For years, I have carried this silver dollar with me as a sign and reminder of the need to share my possessions with those in need.

In a seminary chapel, all present are welcomed to the table to share the bread and the cup. The communion prayer begins by a collective retelling of the story of Jesus' life and death. Following this summary, one of the presiders offers an extended prayer that focuses on Jesus' solidarity with the poor. He calls on the Spirit to enliven us with lives that bear the mark of Christ. As he prays, he quickly walks down the aisle and pushes open the doors of the chapel. "These doors must be open so that all non-documented people can participate in this meal."[10] Here communion is marked by an awareness of those who are not present and whom we often exclude without any acknowledgement of the way our communities ignore and marginalize

9. Collaborative Ministry Office at Creighton University, "Remembering Archbishop Oscar Romero."

10. From a service at Union (NY) seminary, Cláudio Carvalhaes presiding.

them. As we are welcomed to the table to eat and drink, we remember those who are not present with us around the table.

In recent years, larger church gatherings have found that communion services can help them negotiate difficult debates. Denominations facing highly contested social issues have discovered that gathering at the table at the start of the meeting increases the possibility for dialogue and respectful debate. Those who begin by recognizing Christ's claim on our lives and our unity at the table are more likely to recognize that our theological and doctrinal differences are not enough to cause us to denounce one another.[11] *At a Presbytery meeting where an important vote on ordination standards was planned, those planning worship provided an opening communion service that emphasized the unity of the body of Christ. All came forward to receive the elements as a sign of our commitment to follow Christ. The debate that followed the service was heated, but respectful. We all discovered that those who break bread together and share the cup find it more difficult to vilify the opponent during debates. Our unity in Christ supersedes our differences of opinion.*

Each of these brief descriptions presents a way that the outline of Christ's life, death, and resurrection provides a shape to the service and a way to live out these claims on our lives. At stake in these prayers at the table are basic Christian virtues of hospitality, compassion, acceptance, and an openness to the Spirit's transformation of our lives and our community.

VOICES OF ACCLAMATION

How will we respond to these opportunities and challenges? Once we have heard the story of God's persistent love for us and for all the world and once we have been offered the pattern of Christ's life, we are invited to join in a response that affirms this shape as a model for the renewal of our own lives.

In many eucharistic prayers, the primary response is known as the great acclamation. The presider expresses deep awe of God's involvement in the redemption of creation with the words: "Great is the mystery of the faith." The people are invited to respond:

"Christ has died.

---

11. Worship leaders must show caution in planning these services in order that the Lord's Supper is not used as a source of manipulation to hold a church group together. Instead, the table can serve as a starting point for lively and animated discussion that may not lead to agreement, but does not lead to a point of rupture.

Christ is risen.
Christ will come again."

These words offer worshipers a way to articulate the shape of Christ's life that is grounded in the incarnation, resurrection, and the hope of Christ's return. Repetition of this central mystery of the Christian faith is a kind of participation in itself. By expressing this summary, we as worshipers seek to take this pattern of self-giving as part of our lives in the hope and belief that God will bring new life to us.

LASTING REFLECTIONS

The confirmation class of three teenage boys gathered around my dining room table. On the table was a communion chalice, a bowl of water, and a Bible. Soon, we would add the pizza for dinner. Each week we gathered to study ways that Word and Sacrament shape our lives. On this occasion, we were talking about the role of water in baptism. I asked the boys about ways water is used in our lives. There were the usual answers: drinking water, showering, playing in it. Then one young man said that in the Middle Ages water was used as a mirror in order to see reflections of one's self. This image of seeing ourselves in the water of baptism has stuck with me through the years. In a similar way, the Eucharistic Prayer with its portrait of Christ provides an image and model for the shape of our lives. Coming to the table becomes a way of looking again into the mirror of Christ's life to see ways to conform our lives to this image of service, compassion, and self-giving.
In the final analysis, coming to the table is about offering ourselves in thanksgiving for God's grace. As the outline of the gospel is faithfully proclaimed and as the assembly offers its voice of acclamation, we are invited to respond in faith. Each time we gather at the table, we grow toward the goal of taking on the pattern of Christ's life in our own lives. Throughout this chapter, the conversations about sacrifice at the table have been reframed in order to help us realize that God's past actions are not a substitute for the call on our lives. At the table, through the images from Christ's self-giving, we are invited to offer ourselves as a holy offering in service to God's redemptive work in the world.

7

Reexamining our Sacramental Language and Practices

A PRIMARY PART OF re-forming liturgical theology is to look carefully at our words and actions when we gather for worship. Here pastors and theologians are tasked with testing the question of coherence within the broad scope and framework of the ritual action. Do the words and actions come together in ways that make clear claims that participants can follow? How does the ritual provide a map for regular participants (insiders) and how does it make room for newcomers (outsiders) to navigate their way through the activities? Once again, I will seek direction from the work of the analytical philosopher Ludwig Wittgenstein who sought to clear up problems within the way that we use language. Wittgenstein described the work of philosophy as untying knots or bringing clarity to the logic of arguments that were made. Wittgenstein explained this process with these words:

> Language sets everyone the same traps; it is an immense network of easily accessible wrong turnings. And so we watch one man after another walking down the same paths and we know in advance where he will branch off, where walk straight on without noticing the side turning, etc. etc. What I have to do then is erect signposts at all the junctions where there are wrong turnings so as to help people past the danger points.[1]

1. Wittgenstein, *Culture and Value*, 18c.

Thus, I want to press the questions: How can liturgy avoid wrong turns? Where do we need to put up signposts in order to help participants live into the claims of the gospel on our lives that the liturgy seeks to make? The task of theology is to carefully analyze our rituals in order to point to places where our language and actions fall short of providing clear patterns for our lives.

FIRST STEPS: A BRIEF ANALYSIS

As an example of this kind of investigative work, I turn my attention to the opening section of the Eucharistic Prayer (A) as found in the *Book of Common Worship* (BCW) of the Presbyterian Church (U.S.A.). While this specific language may be unique to Presbyterians, the questions that I am raising are applicable to eucharistic prayers and practices in other ecclesial bodies. For Presbyterians, a standard introduction to the eucharistic rite is the Invitation to the Table:

> This is the joyful feast of the people of God.
> People will come from North and South and East and West
> to sit at table in the kingdom of God.
> This is the Lord's table.
> Our Lord invites all who trust in him to eat this feast
> which he has prepared.[2]

I listen to these words from the *Book of Common Worship* on a regular basis. Over the years, they have begun to bother me on a number of levels, so I begin this analysis with a critique of the use of language. By examining our vocabulary, I hope to point out the kind of incongruities that those of us in the church have grown comfortable with and accustomed to hearing.

A careful examination of our language and practices allows us to see places of incongruity—blind spots—where our words and actions fail to convey what we think that they do. This will allow us to clear room in order to more closely align our rituals with what we hope they will accomplish. This is particularly important in this era of post-Christendom as we seek to welcome those who have rarely or never participated in our worship services. At stake in this brief (and admittedly idiosyncratic) assessment is the desire to open up space in our language and rituals so that regular participants see connections to daily life more clearly and so that visitors

---

2. Presbyterian Church (U.S.A.), *Book of Common Worship*, 68.

and newcomers to our gatherings have a clearer sense of what we are doing. So let us look briefly at four questions that are raised in light of the typical words and actions that are often a part of the eucharistic prayers that I hear.

1. Where's the Joy?

Seldom do I see joy on the face of the presider or on the faces of the people who have come to worship. More often than not, I hear these words read/ droned by the presider, and I look around the sanctuary and see people leafing through orders of worship, hoping that the service will end quickly. We may call it a joyful feast all we want, but it rarely appears to convey this emotional mood. Is it a kind of moral imperative that we are supposed to feel joyful when we come to the table? Are we supposed to stay away if we feel other emotions? I wonder how those who grew up outside the church respond when they wander into our sanctuary to visit one of our services. Is this just another example of the way that Christian language remains completely out of touch with our actual feelings and surroundings?

2. Where's the Feast?

Even when I overlook the claim of joy, I get stuck on the "feast" language. There on the altar is a small pile of wafers or a loaf of bread (or sometimes a tray of croutons) next to a small pitcher of wine or juice. When did a bite of bread and a sip of wine become a feast? Or as some have claimed, is it an eschatological use of language in expectation of a future banquet (one that hopefully has more and better food and drink!)? Even in congregations that have worked to restore more robust communion practices, one receives a large piece of bread to dip into a chalice. While this is certainly a step in the right direction, it is not a feast. If we approach this act of eating as a vow or promise (an ancient understanding of the word "sacrament"), then let us at least work to clarify that this is a pledge to feed the hungry. Instead, we find ourselves perplexed and bewildered by the common claims of language and its lack of connection to the ritual objects that are present.

3. Why Is It the Lord's Table?

Why do we insist on calling it the "Lord's table"? I understand that this is an attempt to underscore the theological conviction that it is the risen Christ who meets us as we gather to break bread and drink wine. And yet, according to Scripture, it is this same risen Christ who meets us on the road to Emmaus (Luke 24) and on the seashore (John 21). For the truth is that all our tables and all our lives belong to Christ. So why not simply welcome and invite us to encounter Christ in this particular place at this particular time with this particular group of people? Nothing irks me more these days than the pastors who add a further disclaimer: This is not a Presbyterian or a Methodist table; this is the Lord's table. It causes me to wonder: Is there something wrong with Presbyterian tables? Can Methodists not practice hospitality from the tables in their sanctuaries? Furthermore, our insistence on labeling this as the Lord's table exacerbates the tendency to treat this table in the church completely differently than the other tables around which we gather. The special table with a minimum of food and drink is the Lord's table, whereas the other tables where we gather for hearty meals and celebrations are our own tables. Surely, we need to find ways to show the connection between these tables in order that the grace we encounter and receive will transform our own meal practices.

4. Couldn't the Lord Prepare a Better Spread?

Finally, if we are going to attribute this meager meal to the Lord's work, then couldn't the Lord prepare a better meal than a bite of squishy bread and a sip of wine or Welch's grape juice? As we will see when we examine the earliest Christian meal gatherings, the problems were not about a minimalistic amount of food, but instead about the difficulty of sharing equally. For those who insist on maintaining the language of the Lord's table, then at the very least the elements and distribution need to connote abundance. Additionally, the language of the Lord's table fails to recognize the work of those in the congregation, usually women, who come early and work in the kitchen to prepare the elements for the communion services. In what ways can we acknowledge the gifts and commitments of those who make our gatherings possible?

When we step back from our liturgies and listen to them with the ears of a newcomer or examine our gestures and actions, then we can discover how confusing these words and actions must be to those who do not take them for granted or who have been habituated into their patterns. Here, careful analysis and thoughtful reflection can provide a starting point for considering ways to renew our rituals.

CLUES FOR MOVING FORWARD: RECONNECTING OUR WORDS AND ACTIONS

Given this analysis of places where our language and actions point in odd and confusing directions and fail to communicate basic patterns for living as disciples of Jesus Christ, where can we turn to find ways to realign our eucharistic gatherings? First, let us examine what is at stake in this process. The word "eucharist" simply means thanksgiving, so a core goal is to cultivate a practice of giving thanks in the lives of participants. Learning and practicing gratitude for the gift of grace, of one another, of food and drink, and of life itself is a primary goal of eucharistic prayer. At the center of eucharistic prayer and practice is a gathering of Christians to share a meal with each other (and those who are poor) and cultivate the practice of expressing gratitude to God for the gifts that sustain our lives. Here, we see that the Eucharist is not simply about providing a sacred moment somehow apart and disconnected from the rest of our lives. It is about the work of the Spirit that allows us to encounter Christ's presence in the gift of bread, wine, and one another in order that we may rediscover our dependence on God's grace for every moment in life. Thomas O'Loughlin notes the tragic consequences of a eucharistic theology that, as it developed, became an increasingly separate ritual from daily life: "there was a severing of the event of the Eucharist and Christians' normal course of living; and this fissure took practical expression in that 'taking communion' became in most churches a rare event for the 'ordinary people' and this was not seen as problematic by pastors or theologians."[3]

A preliminary step is to look back to the historical sources about the development of eucharistic practice in order to discern ways that we can realign our liturgies that will reinvigorate our discipleship.

3. O'Loughlin, *Eucharist*, 97–98.

1. Biblical Roots

Clearly, this is not the occasion for a lengthy study of meal practices in the New Testament. Instead, I want to point to common ingredients in two foundational texts that underscore two basic components in the basic practices in the early Christian communities.

Luke depicts the church's rapid growth following Pentecost as centered around basic meal practices. It is worth noting that the initial growth of this movement is associated with a harvest festival of the spring wheat (Shavuot, or Pentecost as it is known in Greek, for occurring fifty days after Passover). To celebrate this festival, Jews gathered in Jerusalem from around the ancient world to give thanks for the harvesting of the grain (as well as the giving of the Torah). The celebration was in thanks for the bounty of the land that provided wheat, barley, grapes, figs, pomegranates, olives, and dates (Deut 8:8). The provisions for this occasion are noted in Deuteronomy 26, where the offering of the first fruits of the harvest are dedicated to give thanks for God's faithfulness. Here, it is important for our purposes to note that the celebration of this festival centered around food and drink. Thus, the Jews who were in Jerusalem following the crucifixion of Jesus, and who heard and responded to the sermon of Peter that Jesus was the fulfillment of God's promise, were those who had come to mark the occasion by giving thanks for God's faithfulness by offering the first fruits of the harvest. There amidst the bounty of food and drink, the proclamation of the kerygma took root and began to spread quickly. In this context, note how Luke depicts the initial results of this nascent group. In memory and thanksgiving for the ways that Yahweh provided for their ancestors, these first followers of Jesus pooled their resources in order to provide for any who were in need. They devoted themselves to prayer and the teachings of the apostles. "Day by day, as they spent much time together in the temple, they broke bread at home and ate their food with glad and generous hearts" (Acts 2:46). The sharing of their food was a central practice that defined this new community. Note as well that Luke uses his signature language of "breaking bread," which throughout his Gospel and Acts is characteristic of the meal gatherings around Jesus (e.g., feeding of the 5,000 and Jesus' final meal with his disciples in the upper room).

In a second text that includes an early description of eucharistic practice (1 Cor 12), the Apostle Paul writes to the church at Corinth about what he has heard in regards to their gatherings. At the communal meals, conflict has erupted due to the inequity of sharing between the wealthy and the poor in the congregation. Some members are bringing lavish meals and gorging themselves on food and wine, whereas others arrive late and have little to eat or drink. Indeed the description of the food at this gathering sounds much more like potlucks in most churches today than it does like most current eucharistic practice, with a bite of bread or wafer and a sip of wine or juice. Note that the critique that Paul offers is not about the amount of food and drink that is present. Rather, he is concerned about the unwillingness of those who have abundance to share with those who have little. In fact, his indictment against the Corinthian community is that their failure to share food and wine with those in need is what leads to his claim that their practice is not in line with the values of the Lord's Supper.[4] Paul's command for the Corinthians to examine themselves in regards to their worthiness to participate in this meal is directly linked to his analysis of their reputed unwillingness to share their food and drink with others in their community, particularly those who were in need.[5]

These seminal texts in Acts and 1 Corinthians underscore that Christian meal gatherings in the name and memory of Jesus included: 1) significant amounts of food and drink; and 2) a willingness to share with one's neighbor and those in need. These defining characteristics lie at the core of eucharistic practice throughout the early development of the Christian movement. To these texts we might add the description of the practice in sources like the Didache, in which the communal gathering includes the sharing of (daily) bread and a collection for those who were in need.

2. Greco-Roman Meals

The recognition of the centrality of food in the early Christian gatherings has been strengthened by the emergence of a growing body of research that claims that early Christian meal practices drew heavily on the patterns of the Greco-Roman banquets. New Testament scholars have reexamined the meal stories throughout the New Testament and discovered significant parallels between the description of banquets in Hellenistic literature and the language and images of the meal descriptions in the Gospels.[6] This re-

---

4. For an analysis of the use of language of the "Lord's Supper," see McGowan, "Myth of the 'Lord's Supper,'" 502–20.

5. Galbreath, *Leading from the Table*, 20ff.

6. See Smith, *From Symposium to Eucharist* and Taussig, *In the Beginning was the Meal*.

search shows that a burgeoning meal practice was at the center of Jesus' public ministry. The descriptions of the guests reclining, the significance of seating arrangements at the meals, the questions about inclusion and exclusion, the roles of hosts and guests—all these common motifs in the meal stories in the Gospels show marked similarities with the depictions of banquets throughout the ancient Greco-Roman world. Recent analysis of the Greco-Roman banquet literature has developed a list of values and ideals that are markedly similar to the discussion of values of the reign of God in the New Testament: for instance, *koinonia*, equality, good order, and joy.[7] While certainly distinctions can be drawn between the early Christian meal practices and the banquet practices of other groups, an awareness of the likelihood that Christian eucharistic practice drew heavily from these patterns further reinforces the centrality of food at the center of Christian gatherings. Early Christian communities worked out their identity, commitment, and beliefs while gathered around tables filled with food and drink. The meal was a central defining practice in the establishment and maintenance of their communities.

3. Historical Development

While a meal setting provided the community with a basic way to gather, these meals took on different forms in different parts of the ancient world. The Greco-Roman banquet tradition provided a rough template that could be adapted to the needs of different communities. Recent research on Christian meal practices shows one constant: diversity was the norm. In some places, full meals remained a regular feature of Christian life. In other places, the practice was modified, likely to meet the demands of working people within the community. In this case, a regular daily meal of bread and water (and wine if available) maintained the communal gathering around food and drink (as well as the collection and distribution to those in need).

Early Christian worship adapted to a variety of local and cultural influences that shaped the way the Christians gathered to tell stories and memories of Jesus and to share a common meal in their worship gatherings. Paul Bradshaw has described the variety of food that was used in meals in different Christian meal gatherings in the early centuries of the

7. See the essays by Klinghardt, "A Typology of the Communal Meal" and Smith, "Greco-Roman Banquet." See also my discussion of these themes in *Leading into the World*.

church. Eucharistic meals ran a wide gamut from full meals, like the one described in 1 Corinthians 11, to simple meals of bread and water. Bradshaw cites evidence that communion meals included oil, bread, vegetables, salt, cheese, and milk and honey.[8] Diversity of practice, particularly in different geographic areas, was normative and valued. Communion in North Africa likely looked quite different from the gatherings in Antioch. This diversity in practice lasted for four centuries in the Western church until the powers in Rome required greater conformity in the church's liturgy. In fact, it was not until 393 CE that the Synod of Hippo passed a rule that stipulated that only bread and wine mixed with water were allowed on the communion table.[9]

From these diverse meal gatherings at the formative center of early Christian communities, we can slowly trace the devolution/disappearance of shared meals to a ritual that was marked by a minimalization of food and drink as well as an increasing tendency to view the practice primarily in terms of spiritual categories. Thomas O'Loughlin charts these developments and concludes:

> The practical irony is that the Eucharist is built around eating and drinking, uses the human grammar of meals, items of food and expressed itself in language that is well located in the human world. But, once it comes to practical expression, it is not a meal in any real sense compared with the ways we take part in a meal whether that is the simplest shared meal or a special banquet.[10]

Instead of a shared meal around a table with provisions for those who are in need, the ritual largely became a "token affair"[11] with the goal of prompting observing participants to reflect on Christ's death long ago.

Given the historical development away from experiencing the Eucharist as a meal, Christian communities today face the challenge of reclaiming and reinvigorating our practices in ways that show clearer connections between our Sunday gatherings and our daily lives. Lessons from the early Christian meal practices can serve as an important guide in this task of renewal.

---

8. Bradshaw, *Eucharistic Origins*, 59.

9. Bieler and Schottroff, *Eucharist*, 115. It is worth noting that the passing of a rule does not necessarily mean that all communities immediately followed it.

10. O'Loughlin, *Eucharist*, 147.

11. O'Loughlin, *Eucharist*, 148.

THE ROAD TO RECOVERY: TOWARDS
A TENTATIVE CONCLUSION

In the twentieth century, the liturgical renewal movement made great strides at reclaiming certain aspects of the centrality of Eucharist as a part of regular Christian gatherings. Much has been accomplished by these efforts, including significant revisions to worship resources, the widespread use of fuller eucharistic prayers, and a dramatic increase in communion frequency. And yet, eucharistic practice remains largely disconnected from the daily lives of most Christians. For those who visit our gatherings, the Eucharist remains an odd, other-worldly ritual that runs contrary to the common language of food and sharing that we use. Here, the church faces the call to reexamine and realign our practices with our lives as disciples of Jesus Christ. As O'Loughlin concludes, "If the evidence of the early churches, and their memories of Jesus, have any value for Christians today, then Christians need to see a blessing as a part of every meal, and having a meal together as central to their common worship."[12]

One place to start is by changing our visions and expectations. A congregation that I visited in Managua, Nicaragua, commissioned a mural for the background of the platform in their simple building. Each week as the priest celebrated the Mass with the congregation, images of abundant bread, fruit, and flowers filled the space (along with striking images of women and famous revolutionary leaders).

At Union Presbyterian Seminary, we have reclaimed the vision of a fuller table life together. Students refer to the services where I preside as "cheese eucharist" since in addition to the bread and cup, fruit and cheese are added to the offerings on the table. We practice extending the table by gathering around it to share the bounty of food as a precursor to our community-wide lunch. It's a small step, yet an important move beyond the morsel of bread and sip of juice that has defined our communion practice.

Other communities are charting more dramatic ways of living into this future. In *Take This Bread*, Sara Miles chronicled her own conversion experience in creating a feeding program linked to the eucharistic practices around the altar at St. Gregory of Nyssa in San Francisco. At St. Lydia's in Brooklyn, New York, the community gathers around tables for "Dinner Church" on Sunday and Monday evenings. These communities and others are finding ways to reclaim the vision of shared meals from the early church.

12. O'Loughlin, *Eucharist*, 156.

On this journey, there is no prescriptive list that will work in all congregations. Instead, we will reclaim the diversity of practices that marked the early Christian communities.

As we reclaim the central place of food and drink in our gatherings, it is important to keep the vision of providing for those in need at the center of our assemblies. We will always be tempted in this consumerist culture to simply serve ourselves, but the vision that we have discovered from the early church is one in which Christian communities provided food to widows, orphans, prisoners, and those in need. So as we work to restore meal practices to our communities, let us also pledge to link this to providing food for those in our neighborhoods who are hungry. As we continue the work of liturgical renewal, it is important to look for wrong turns that creep into our rituals. By realigning our words and actions, we can reclaim the eucharistic vision and practice of the early church as we gather around the table as followers of Jesus to share food and drink with all who hunger and thirst.

PART THREE

The Earth as Guide for Our Future

WE LIVE IN A time of crisis: environmental, political, economic, ecclesial. Everywhere we turn these days, we are confronted by crises of epic proportions. Media stokes our anxieties by generating non-stop coverage of the latest disaster that we face. In the midst of these dilemmas, the church seems to have largely lost its voice. Mainline denominations continue to face decline in membership and resources. Christian life has increasingly moved out of the public arena as faith is relegated to personal spaces that are defined in terms of vague, private spiritual categories. Yet the crises that we face are of a shared, social nature. How will we respond collectively to the environmental changes that are wreaking havoc in terms of climate change and toxic contamination to our water and soil? How will we come together as humans to confront the political challenges of white supremacy and other forms of racial discrimination? How will we learn to share our resources equitably so that the poor can be lifted out of their daily struggle to survive?

Now is a critical time for Reformed Christians to rediscover what we have to offer in terms of modeling ways to meet the global challenges that we face with our neighbors. How can our experience and understanding of the gospel prompt us to respond to the crises around us? How will we maintain hope in a time of cynicism and despair? In the following three essays, I explore ways that the earth can teach us to live in harmony and balance. The first essay in this section explores how a broader, ecumenical appropriation of sacramentality that draws on incarnational language helps us reclaim a vision of the earth as a place of encounter with the divine. This transition pushes the church to move beyond its walls in order to experience ways in which the earth provides the resources and places for us to see our lives in light of God's presence in one another and in the world around us.

The next essay offers a particular model for connecting Christian discipleship with earth care. Recognizing and commissioning those among us who are exercising a heightened commitment to respond to the environmental crises that we are facing offers a significant way for congregations to encourage and foster practices that link Christian identity with the call to respond to the suffering that we see in the world around us. These forms of service take their cues from the testimony of Scripture that creation itself groans in labor and waits for redemption (Rom 8:22). Here, Christians join with others in the work for the liberation of the earth as a particular way of living out our baptismal vows to care for God's creation.

The last essay in this section examines how new liturgical resources that draw on the richness of earth images can reinvigorate our worship services. The renewal and reorientation of our worship takes its cues from the richness of Scripture and the incarnational signs of the earth as the place of God's presence. Special attention to the language and embodiment of our baptismal rites provides an important step in seeing our connection to the earth. Finally, three brief homilies show ways of connecting our reading of Scripture with our call to care for the earth.

8

Tracing the Sacramental Circle

In this chapter, I seek to briefly reexamine the role of the sacraments in the Reformed tradition in order to propose a way to reconcile the division that the great Roman Catholic liturgical theologian Louis-Marie Chauvet described between sacramental and non-sacramental approaches to theology. This division has often been characterized by a primary focus on Scripture and preaching in Protestant congregations and a historic emphasis on the celebration of the mass in the Roman Catholic Church.[1] I hope to make the case for a new approach to this question by reexamining this relationship in light of the pressing need for the church to respond to the environmental crises that we are facing.

Along the way, I will draw guidance from the historic, ecumenical document *Baptism, Eucharist and Ministry*, adopted by the World Council of Churches at its meeting in Lima, Peru, in 1982 and the responses to this document by those in faith communities, before turning to the emergence of the environmental movement and a growing body of eco-theological literature that is contributing to a reexamination of the church's practices and ethical commitments. In this brief sketch, I hope to point to ways that these movements have contributed to a potential for liturgical renewal that can help us move from an ego-centered to an eco-centered theology (in the words of ethicist Larry Rasmussen).

1. Note how Vatican II sought to correct this pattern among Roman Catholics by calling for the opening up of the riches of Scripture to the assembly. Similarly, mainline Protestants have sought to recover a balance between Word and Table in the weekly worship life of faith communities.

PART 1: A BRIEF ANALYSIS OF REFORMED ROOTS

In the conclusion of his classic work *Symbol and Sacrament*, Chauvet proposes a theology of sacramentality that draws from the world as creation. Chauvet writes: "Sacraments present the world to us as something that we may not use in an arbitrary fashion; they demand that we make of reality a 'world' for all, and not simply for the well-off. . . . They reveal to us the 'sacramentality' of the world as creation."[2] Chauvet contrasts this approach with what he calls the non-sacramental theology of Karl Barth, whose christocentric theology seems to leave little room for a Reformed theology that allows the sacraments to be sources, encounters, or means of grace.

In his recent book, *A Touch of the Sacred*, the Dutch Reformed theologian Gerrit Immink draws attention to the significance of relating faith to everyday life as a primary concern and motivating factor of the Protestant Reformation. Immink highlights changes in the role of music and prayer in Calvin's congregations in Strasbourg and Geneva as two key areas to make this point. Congregational singing, especially of the Psalms, marked a particular commitment to participation by the assembly with the expressed hope that these songs would be sung not only in church but would also cultivate a deeper sense of piety in the daily lives of participants. Similarly, a shift from personal to corporate prayer provided a pattern for house prayers and daily devotions. Note, for example, the shift in the prayer of confession from the priest's preparatory prayer before the celebration of the Mass to the congregation's prayer before hearing the reading of Scripture. Calvin, among other Reformers, saw this as an important pattern for cultivating practices of daily devotions among the faithful.

In Zurich, Ulrich Zwingli reoriented eucharistic practice by placing a table in the middle of the sanctuary around which members gathered. To make the case more clearly, Zwingli abandoned the ornate eucharistic vessels in favor of wooden cups. In this drastic shift, the hope was to relate the celebration of the Lord's Supper to meal gatherings at other tables. Ironically, while Zwingli and Calvin tried to develop an approach to the sacraments that showed connections to daily life, their over-reliance on spiritual language and categories made this effort challenging. To underscore this point, note how the shift in the Reformed tradition from the language of the Mass and the altar to that of the Lord's Supper and table ended up denoting a particular table (the one in the church) and thereby undermined

2. Chauvet, *Symbol and Sacrament*, 553.

a sense of connection to other tables.[3] Similarly, the inability to recover a weekly celebration of Word and Table in most Reformed churches limited the connections between table gatherings in church and those in homes and other locations.

To animate the project of connecting corporate worship to daily life, Immink argues persuasively for the distinctive theological commitment to the role of the Holy Spirit as the animating force of the Reformed tradition (and here I would note that there is another interesting parallel with Chauvet's emphasis on pneumatology). Here, the role of epiclesis provides the groundwork for each element of worship. This begins with the unique role of the Prayer for Illumination that calls on the Spirit in order that the reading and proclamation of Scripture may come alive in the assembly and extends through other aspects of worship. Immink also underscores the significant role of the epiclesis in baptism and the Lord's Supper, as well as in other forms of prayer. This leads him to conclude that: "The Protestant tradition connects the Holy Spirit with people and the inner life, rather than with institutions."[4] While I am intrigued by the way he contrasts the role of the epiclesis over and against what he sees as the crucial moment of consecration in the Mass, I am more reluctant to accept his category of "inner life" when surely it is the Spirit in the midst of the community that connects and draws us together as beloved children of God around these things of bread and wine and water and one another. Here, I want to press Immink's language of the Spirit and the inner lives of believers by asking how the biblical narrative of Pentecost in Acts 2 provides a theological foundation for an ecclesiology that is grounded in the Spirit's presence in the actions and responses of the people (rather than in inner spiritual categories). A critical reading of the Acts 2 narrative underscores the way in which the Spirit's presence creates a new community and a shared understanding among those who came from different backgrounds. Here the Acts text offers a theological reversal of the tower of Babel narrative in Genesis 11 by showing the movement from chaos to community that emerges among the early followers of Jesus. It is striking to note how Luke portrays

---

3. It is particularly interesting and troubling to note the disclaimer now given in many Protestant churches that the communion table belongs to the Lord. While the motivation for this announcement is to open the table to those of other denominations, the result of this move is to reinforce the separateness of this table rather than to connect it with other tables around which we gather.

4. Immink, *Touch of the Sacred*, 47.

this as a shared experience rather than as a transformation of the "inner lives" of the participants.

The growing commitment to spiritual presence reinforced the tendency to view the sacraments as other-worldly (here, note the downside of Calvin's contention that the assembly is lifted up to heaven to participate in communion). Over time, Reformed Christians struggled to come to grips with how the elements of the sacraments related to daily life. In its more extreme form, this included the rejection of an epiclesis over the elements as incompatible with a theological understanding of the fallenness of creation.

One can also see the evidence for the lack of sacramental connection to that which surrounds us in the diminishment of the rites and the elements themselves. Over time, the elements themselves continued to shrink until they became little more than a few drops of water at baptism and a crouton and a thimble of grape juice for communion. The sum effect of the Reformation led to what Charles Taylor calls, "excarnation, the transfer of religious life out of bodily forms of ritual, worship, and practice, so that it becomes more and more to reside 'in the head.'"[5] The stuff of creation remains barely visible in lieu of a form of spirituality that is prompted by intellectual reflection on the symbolic meaning of these events.

PART 2: PATHS FORWARD

Given this dilemma, I want to point briefly to two theological movements influencing the broader church to reclaim a connection between the ways that we worship, the urgent need to care for creation, and the importance of relating faith to our daily lives.

Over thirty years ago, the historic, ecumenical document *Baptism, Eucharist and Ministry* (BEM), organized by the World Council of Churches, outlined shared approaches to these practices by diverse ecclesial bodies. While BEM gave more attention to the theological meanings attached to these practices, it nevertheless pointed to common actions and embodied practices in faith communities.

In terms of baptismal practice, BEM pointed to the significant role of water (albeit qualified in terms of the "symbolic dimension of water") as well as the act of laying on hands, and chrismation or anointing. Similarly, the agreement on Eucharist affirmed the centrality of eating and drinking by the assembly.

5. Taylor, *A Secular Age*, 613.

Looking back at BEM after all these years, these declarations may seem like modest steps forward, yet at the time they represented a watershed moment in terms of recognizing common practices between faith communities. A follow-up report to BEM called for further study of the ethical implications of the sacraments, specifically that there was a need for:

> The cosmological dimension of the sacraments [to] be further studied taking into account the material elements used in the sacraments (representing creation and human labour), and the fact that sacraments touch and are touched by all aspects of human life.[6]

It is at this very point that attention to the environmental crises that we face provides an important connection and corrective to the church's theology and practice. Many religious communities have been slow to join the movement and link Christian theology and faith to earth care. In his important work from 1972, *Is it too Late?: A Theology of Ecology*, John Cobb was one of the initial prominent voices urging the church to take up this work.

And yet more than forty years after Cobb's appeal, worship books and resources continue to give limited attention to the prominent place of the earth in Scripture and to the desperate need to connect the life of faith with earth care. Or as Dieter Hessel writes,

> theologians of the church need to give explicit attention to the environmental aspects of biblical narratives, ethical teachings, confessions of faith, the sacraments of baptism and holy communion, and hymns and prayers. With this new sensibility, Christian worship resources need to be reassessed and revised.[7]

In recent days, the environmental movement as well as faith communities have learned the significance of the phrase, "Thinking Globally, Acting Locally." The focus turns to the local and particular. This congregation, with these unique gifts, in this particular place strives to give body and voice to the ways that it connects to the lives of those around us and to this particular piece of the earth.

This means that spiritual-moral formation is irreducibly concrete and local, even when it is the formation of a shared Earth ethic. It happens person by person, congregation by congregation, institution by institution, system by system. And it happens by way of multiple points of entry and

---

6. World Council of Churches, *Baptism, Eucharist and Ministry*, 146.

7. Hessel, "Church Ecologically Reformed," 203.

multiple means as expressed by the whole people of God—young and old, lettered and unlettered, male and female, of whatever race, class, nationality, or ecclesial tradition.[8]

There is widespread agreement about the severity of the current ecological crisis as it relates not only to issues of climate change, but equally significant factors like carbon footprints and sustainability. Thomas Berry refers to the task of global eco-justice as "the Great Work" of our time.[9] This work, according to Paul Santmire, includes "a plethora of global communities and constituencies as it will necessarily have to do: the envisioning and the establishing of a truly just and beautifully viable earth community."[10] In this global context, it is incumbent upon faith communities to contribute our voices and provide responses to the ecological demands of our time that are rooted in our identity as followers of Jesus Christ. Santmire concludes, "Christians today must be radically realistic, radically committed to telling the whole truth, because nothing less than the future of the world God sent Jesus Christ to save—more specifically, the future of life as we know it on Planet Earth—is at stake."[11] Similarly, Larry Rasmussen calls for Christian communities to adapt their teachings and practices in order to address the ecological crisis that we are facing and offer a constructive theology that deals with questions of nature and culture "so as to prevent their destruction and contribute to their sustainability."[12]

While ecclesial bodies and theologians continue to address the importance of the church's response to issues of the ecological crisis, Santmire underscores the need for the church's liturgy to reflect this pressing priority, claiming that a primary task is "to encourage and to help the ecumenical churches, especially those that take the liturgy as a historic given, to renew their worship, precisely in order to make possible more meaningful, more effective, and more passionate Christian participation in the quest to accomplish the Great Work of our time."[13]

We cannot address the issues of climate change and environmental degradation individually. In fact, our involvement in the global economies of scale continues to contribute to the escalating crisis that our planet faces.

8. Rasmussen, "Eco-Justice," 18.

9. Berry, *Great Work*, 391–92.

10. Santmire, *Ritualizing Nature*, 24.

11. Santmire, *Ritualizing Nature*, 8.

12. Rasmussen in Santmire, *Ritualizing Nature*, 25.

13. Santmire, *Ritualizing Nature*, 25.

Our individual choices will not fix the problems that our planet is facing. Nor can the church as communities of individuals address the environmental crisis. Instead, congregations can join with other environmental organizations in order to practice alternative ways of living and caring for the earth.

In the Pacific Northwest, where environmental concern and activism has been prominent for several decades, there are a myriad of agencies and non-profits providing literature, support, gatherings, and forms of connecting with others with similar concerns. While organizations like Earth Ministry in Seattle continue to provide important services, many congregations have yet to show how individual and communal practices of earth care relate to the life of discipleship. There remains a deep hunger for the church to recognize their ongoing commitment to diverse practices of earth care as well as a longing for their congregation to become more proactive in providing resources (in particular biblical/spiritual materials) and modeling ways of integrating Christian faith and earth care.

Further complicating these efforts is the role of a generic spirituality that pervades the broader culture and challenges the nascent attempts of people of faith to claim particular perspectives or rationale for their involvement in earth care. This vague notion of spirituality runs the risk of unintentionally reinforcing the church's own tendency of adopting a language of spirituality that fails to build on an incarnational theology and ultimately devalues the material stuff at the center of the church's assembly.

I witnessed this sense of deep connection to the earth with a vague sense of spirituality during the sabbatical research that I did in the Pacific Northwest where I worked with members of six congregations over the course of a year. I was struck by the common expressions of commitment to and love for the earth that I heard from members in both conservative and progressive congregations that I visited in Oregon, Washington, and British Columbia. While these communities differed significantly in terms of their interpretation of Scripture, theological values, and commitment to social issues, they shared in common a deep and at times mystical sense of the role and beauty of nature. In *Cascadia: The Elusive Utopia*, fourteen authors from a broad range of disciplines describe their spirituality in terms of a connection to nature that people in this region share. One contributor qualifies this understanding: "But, in Cascadia, in the Pacific Nation, we prefer spirituality to religion. We like to be breathed into, as they say, inspired."[14]

In my conversations with people in congregations who were deeply committed to environmental activism, I noted the pervasive way that this language permeated their own descriptions. In these cases, people expressed a deep appreciation for God's presence in creation and a commitment to care for creation, but they generally lacked any form of Christian framework or theological vocabulary to articulate how this related to faith. In conversation with predominantly Anglo congregations, the ethical commitment often relied on the language of the Sierra Club or other organizations working to address environmental concerns. When pressed on theological connections for their actions, participants often resorted to vague claims about the earth as God's creation and our responsibility to care for it. In contrast, two racial-ethnic congregations adopted theological vocabulary from other spiritual frameworks to express their commitment to environmental work. A Native American congregation included images on their communion pottery and paraments that drew from their identity in indigenous communities while at the same time the highly evangelical congregation generally described their theological identity in contrast to the spirituality of their indigenous background. Similarly, in an evangelical Cambodian congregation, members drew on Buddhist images of walking lightly on the earth while seeing their theological identity as distinct from their cultural familiarity with Buddhism.

These testimonies are suggestive of a pressing need for Christian communities to articulate connections between our theological beliefs and practices and our commitment to care for the earth. Here, the ongoing work of eco-theologians can provide a basis for calling Christian communities to the serious work of engaging the environmental crisis that we face.

In her recent book *Ask the Beast*, Elizabeth Johnson notes that:

> The developed tradition of sacramental theology teaches that simple material things such as bread and wine, water, oil, the sexual union of marriage, when blessed by the ritual action and prayer of the church, can be bearers of divine grace. This is so, it now becomes clear, because to begin with the whole physical world itself is a primordial sacrament.[15]

14. Bowering, "Cascadia," 266.
15. Johnson, *Ask the Beasts*, 150–51.

Here, the very stuff of the sacraments is seen in relationship to the earth from which it comes: water, bread and wine from the grain and grapes that grow up out of the earth and provide for our nourishment and well-being, all sustained by the ongoing presence of the divine. It is at this point that the classic theological and sacramental language of divine presence can provide an interpretive clue in showing the relationship between the church's gathering around water, bread, and wine and a commitment to work for the renewal of the earth.

Here, the image of tracing the sacramental circle operates with a deep sense of thanksgiving (*eucharistia*) for these things around which we gather in order to cultivate a commitment to care for the earth from which these things come. Or as Roman Catholic theologian Michael Himes writes: "in a world where the loving kindness of God is everywhere present but often overlooked . . . the church's sacraments break through the fog and call attention to this reality. Using embodied things like bread, wine, oil, water, they name and celebrate grace for a moment, thereby allowing divine presence to gain a stronger foothold in our lives."[16]

CONCLUSION

The testimonies of two particular individuals have remained with me as I listened to people seek to articulate ways in which their faith connects with a notion of divine presence in the world around them.

A retired man living on the coast spoke to me of his work over the last decade to restore habitat to land in his area. As a property owner in a subdivision where development stopped, he described his feelings of looking each day at the bulldozed scars of the earth in the lot next to his own. Finally, he felt compelled to buy the property and work for its healing. Over time he brought back natural plants to the land and created paths and places for contemplation and prayer. His description of the pain of the scarred earth, of absence, as well as his adoption of his own religious practices in this space signaled a desire to connect his work more closely with his Christian faith and yet he seemed to lack any vocabulary that enabled him to make these connections.

A Native American elder in the midst of turbulent times in his personal life prayed for work to support his family. His repeated job applications seemed futile. One morning, in an attempt to escape the routine of

16. Johnson, *Ask the Beasts*, 41.

rejection, he set out floating down the river in a canoe. In the middle of the wilderness, he described his cell phone ringing and receiving an offer of a meaningful job. As he offered a prayer of thanksgiving, he witnessed the cedar trees along the banks of the river, bowing before him.

As powerful as these testimonies are, they remain largely absent of biblical, communal, or sacramental language. They are exemplary of the hard work that remains before us in terms of reconnecting theological language, imagery, and practice to our glimpses of divine presence and absence in the world. As we take up this work of fostering a deeper connection between the sacraments and the earth, we can take encouragement from others working in this area. I will briefly cite two works that I have found suggestive:

First, while I have offered a harsh critique of the spiritualization of the Sacrament within the Reformed tradition, the *Directory for Worship*, the constitutional document of my own tradition (Presbyterian Church U.S.A.) claims, "The early Church, following Jesus, took three primary material elements of life—water, bread, and wine—to become basic symbols of offering life to God as Jesus had offered his life."[17] Here remains a central claim about the importance of not neglecting matter, the stuff that we use for baptism and Eucharist.

Second, in a different way, Linda Gibler's beautiful book, *From the Beginning to Baptism*, presents the stuff of baptism in terms of the scientific, biblical, and sacramental history of water, oil, and fire. Her goal is to recover what Gibler calls "a functional cosmology" that "begins with the sacredness of the cosmos and the Earth community and then asks how religious institutions participate with that sacredness."[18] In this vision, the role of sacraments is to show the integral relationship between the church's ritual practice and daily life.

In the end, the goal of this work is to help the church reorient its practices both inside and outside its walls to the gifts, possibilities, and needs of the created world that we confess is the creative work of God. Instead of following the cultural trend of amorphous spiritual language, the church offers embodied practices that draw on the stuff of the earth to mark ourselves as disciples of Jesus Christ. Here, Christians from different ecclesial traditions can learn from Chauvet's profound insight that "Sacraments are the great

17. Presbyterian Church (U.S.A.), *Constitution of the Presbyterian Church (U.S.A.)*, W-1.3033.

18. Gibler, *From the Beginning to Baptism*, xxvi.

symbolic places which attest that the recognition of the grace of creation and the exigency of a counter-gift are inseparable."[19] Thus, reclaiming a sacramental circle that draws from creation and points to creation provides us with a healthy model for integrating our religion, our daily lives, and the needs of the earth. On this point, a renewed Reformed engagement with the sacraments has much to learn from other ecclesial perspectives while also offering a unique perspective of ways in which all of life is imbued with spirituality.[20]

19. Chauvet, *Symbols and Sacrament*, 554.

20. "[According to Calvin] one does not need special places in which to pray. All of life has become an arena of faith and spirituality." Calvin in Dyrness, *Reformed Theology and Visual Culture*, 82. The historic challenge for Reformed theology is to maintain a balance between a recognition of the divine presence in particular places and the rejection of any forms of idolatry.

9

An Eco-Liturgical Experiment in Contextuality

INTRODUCTION

THE NAIROBI STATEMENT ON Worship and Culture that was adopted by the Lutheran World Federation in 1996 has received wide acceptance for the manner in which it seeks to balance competing tensions in the way that worship relates to culture. The document highlights four ways that Christian worship relates dynamically to culture: transculturally, contextually, counter-culturally, and cross-culturally.[1] In the struggle to maintain a balance between worship that is both transcultural and contextual, the Nairobi Statement accepts a given core of Scripture and Sacrament as universally normative for the church. The contextual nature of worship is designated as that which uses elements of local culture "in order to enrich its original core."[2] While the Nairobi Statement ends in a call on churches to recover the transcultural elements of worship as well as explore the contextual elements, the document itself gives priority to those elements which are designated as part of the universal core.

A basic challenge for liturgical scholars is to continue to explore the dynamics between these different elements of worship in order to ensure

1. Lutheran World Federation, *Christian Worship*, 23–28.
2. Lathrop, *Holy People*, 235.

that the local, particular approaches to worship are not suppressed or evis-cerated in an attempt to enforce universal approaches to worship that seek to identify a historic and theological core. Thus, the basic question that this liturgical study explores is: How does one maintain a sense of dynamic bal-ance between these elements? Or to put it a slightly different way: How can the local, contextual elements of worship both challenge and support our hypotheses about universal, transcultural elements of worship?

Background

Recent work in the early history of sacramental practice has led to a grow-ing awareness of the diversity of practices within Christian communities during the early centuries of the church. While weekly Eucharist and bap-tismal initiation were core rituals, they were carried out in distinct ways in different communities. Eucharistic meals ran a wide gamut from full meals (1 Cor 11) to a simple meal of bread and wine mixed with water (as described in the Didache). Some communities included milk and honey in the meal gathering; others used olive oil alongside the bread and wine. "There are also signs that in certain communities other foodstuffs may have accompanied the bread and water (or wine) at the ritual meals and a thanksgiving said over them."[3] Eventually, the Synod of Hippo in 393 CE passed a rule that stipulated that only bread and wine mixed with water were allowed on the communion table.[4]

Similarly, baptismal practices developed diverse patterns. The New Testament includes an assorted selection of images, formulas, and patterns for baptism. Christian baptism was influenced by a wide variety of ritual practices from other religious traditions as well as from Roman bathing customs. After surveying the biblical images, Bryan Spinks concludes:

> The New Testament is both the fulcrum from which emerges all theological reflection on baptism and all Christian baptismal rites, and the touchstone, or "norming norm" against which they may be tested. However, the books of the New Testament present neither a single doctrine of baptism, nor some archetypal liturgical rite.[5]

3. Bradshaw, *Eucharistic Origins*, 59. Bradshaw cites evidence that includes the fol-lowing foods: oil, bread, vegetables, salt, cheese, and milk and honey.

4. Bieler and Schottroff, *Eucharist*, 115. It is worth noting that the passing of a rule does not necessarily mean that all communities immediately followed it.

5. Spinks, *Early and Medieval Rituals*, 12.

There is a growing recognition among scholars that as the Christian movement spread across the Roman Empire, baptismal practice took on distinctive features of local communities. The practices of anointing before and/or after bathing quickly became a customary part of baptism. Local communities likely followed regional cultural customs in their choices of when to anoint the individual and other bathing custom actions that became part of the baptismal liturgy. For example, some Christian communities adopted the use of incense while others used ritual lamps and torches. Over time these ritual elements were given theological interpretations (e.g., oil is for sealing and preservation, or light is for illumination). Spinks concludes his analysis of the documents from the first three centuries: "We find different ritual patterns. . . . Thus the different ritual patterns found in the early Christian evidences mirror secular bathing customs."[6]

As liturgical practice became more generally fixed and prescribed, the diversity of practices often gave way to a normative uniformity. In fact, the emergence of fixed liturgical texts shifted the balance in liturgical practice towards the universal. While local cultural patterns surely continued to influence the liturgical celebration, this shift tipped the balance away from the contextual towards the transcultural.

MODERN LITURGICAL APPROACHES

During the twentieth century, the emergence of the liturgical renewal movement (coupled with the ecumenical movement) pressed scholars to further identify and establish a reducible core shared by the church.[7] In the mid-twentieth century, the classic work of Dom Gregory Dix in *The Shape of the Liturgy* provided a nearly evangelical interpretation of a transhistorical, liturgical core. Dix's thesis on the historical foundation of the Mass and its preservation through history and culture continues to hold influence on the development of liturgical resources that seek to preserve an ecumenical and historical common ground.

Recently, the work of Paul Bradshaw has finally challenged the dominance of Dix's hypothesis.

6. Spinks, *Early and Medieval Rituals*, 35–36.

7. Interestingly, the search for a liturgical core mined the riches of early church history to establish a prototype which was then promulgated through the production of worship books and resources in mainline Protestant denominations.

> So seductive has been the picture painted by Dix that it has tended
> to blind us to its shortcomings and thus mislead us. . . . For the
> truth is that there is no really firm evidence that primitive eucha-
> ristic practice ever did conform to the sevenfold shape of the Last
> Supper, whereas there are signs of the existence of early Christian
> ritual meals that do not seem to relate themselves to this event or
> to be patterned according to its model.[8]

Bradshaw's methodical critique of Dix's historical reconstruction of a uni-
linear transmission of the Mass has been joined by a growing body of work
that underscores the significance of other cultural influences on the meal
practice of early Christian communities, especially the Greco-Roman banquet. In particular, the work of Dennis Smith and Hal Taussig has strengthened the understanding of the diverse influences on the development of
eucharistic practices in the early Christian movement.[9]

While the grip of Dix's hypothesis about the development and preservation of eucharistic prayer is finally beginning to recede, a more nuanced
approach that argues for the recognition and priority of universal elements
throughout the history of Christian worship has taken its place. Gordon
Lathrop follows a similar trajectory as Dix's work in arguing for a universal
shape of the liturgy, which Lathrop identifies as the *ordo*. Lathrop discovers
an implicit grounding of this fourfold pattern (gathering, word, thanksgiving, sending) in Scripture itself. Lathrop proceeds to move beyond merely
recognizing these transcultural elements to arguing for their priority over
contextual practices and local customs.

> We need to require local traditions . . . to take second place to
> thanksgiving at table and the shared holy meal. We need to require
> local traditions to circle around and serve the central matters of
> our communion, the word and sacraments that bear us into the
> very life of the triune God. The church is always local, but the local
> reality must be broken open toward the one who holds all locali-
> ties together and so is the ground of our *koinonia*.[10]

8. Bradshaw, *Eucharistic Origins*, vi.

9. Smith and Taussig published a brief examination of their thesis in *Many Tables:
The Eucharist in the New Testament and Liturgy Today* (1990). Since that time, they have
separately published major works on the influence of Greco-Roman meals on the development of early Eucharistic practice. See Dennis Smith, *From Symposium to Eucharist:
The Banquet in the Early Christian World* (2003) and Hal Taussig, *In the Beginning was
the Meal: Social Experimentation and Early Christian Identity* (2009).

10. Lathrop, *Holy People*, 127. I am not sure whom Lathrop is referencing with the
pronoun "we."

Such an approach presumes a universal core to the thanksgiving at table. Like Dix, Lathrop claims a divine mandate for a liturgical *ordo* that comes as God's gift to the church. Lathrop quotes from the Ditchington Report (which he helped write): "The pattern of this gathering and sending has come to all the churches as a common and shared inheritance. That received pattern resides in the basic outlines of what may be called the *ordo* of Christian worship."[11]

RESPONSE

While many liturgical theologians give lip service to the importance of preserving the tension between the approaches to culture, the primary emphasis often remains on the preservation of what liturgical scholars have identified as the transcultural components of worship to which local, contextual expressions are expected "to take second place."

On this point, Presbyterians may be able to offer a unique perspective. The *Directory for Worship,* which is a part of the church's constitution, describes the ongoing tension between form and freedom in worship.

> The Church has always experienced a tension between form and freedom in worship. In the history of the Church, some have offered established forms for ordering worship in accordance with God's Word. Others, in the effort to be faithful to the Word, have resisted imposing any fixed forms upon the worshiping community. The Presbyterian Church (U.S.A.) acknowledges that all forms of worship are provisional and subject to reformation. In ordering worship the church is to seek openness to the creativity of the Holy Spirit, who guides the church toward worship which is orderly yet spontaneous, consistent with God's Word and open to the newness of God's future. (W-3.1002a)[12]

While the *Directory for Worship* provides a descriptive approach to the elements of worship for Reformed congregations, it holds these elements in a creative tension that acknowledges the defining role of Scripture and sacraments, while avoiding a prescriptive approach that mandates that the elements of worship must be fixed in a particular theological or cultural way. Instead, worship is to remain a place of dynamic exchange as the

11. Lathrop, *Holy People,* 125.

12. Presbyterian Church (U.S.A.), *Constitution of the Presbyterian Church (U.S.A.): Part II, Book of Order.*

tension between form and freedom is exercised in the context of a local congregation.[13]

This approach recognizes the value and benefits of liturgical forms that have been written and developed by leaders of the church while at the same time avoiding the dangers of a hierarchical approach that prescribes and mandates a fixed liturgical schema (such an approach is often accompanied by a rationale that justifies the development of the liturgical texts by historical and theological grounds; for example, note Lathrop's claims of a received liturgical pattern or text). By contrast, the historic approach of the Presbyterian Church is to honor and value the church's development of historic forms for worship while recognizing the transitory quality of these forms. This openness to freedom and spontaneity preserves a fundamental place for contextual elements of worship to provide interpretative experiences for local congregations.

CONTEXTUALITY AS AN IMAGINATIVE EXERCISE

Paying careful attention to the particular interests and needs of a local community of faith allows the liturgist to point to and/or forge new connections between worship and the daily life of the worshipers. This exchange between liturgical form and freedom makes room for an interplay between the expected liturgical patterns of a congregation and particular liturgical expressions that address local concerns. Such an emphasis on contextuality in worship allows the local elements of worship to disrupt and challenge the claims of a universal *ordo*. Imagining new ways of crafting the movements of the liturgy allows the participants to see the world around us in different ways.

As we have previously noted, the philosopher Ludwig Wittgenstein noted the importance of perspective in seeing the world around us in different ways.

> Well, I should like you to say: "Yes, it's true, you can imagine that too, that might happen too!"—But was I trying to draw someone's attention to the fact that he is capable of imagining that?—I wanted to put that picture before him, and his *acceptance* of the picture consists in his now being inclined to regard a given case

13. On this point, I acknowledge that local congregations often fix their own liturgical patterns rather than do the hard work of living within the tension of form and freedom.

differently: that is to compare with *this* rather than *that* set of pictures. I have changed his *way of looking at things.*[14]

In this passage from *Philosophical Investigations*, Wittgenstein stressed the role of perspective as that which allows someone to accept and understand a particular way of looking at the world. This perspective, this way of understanding, is grounded in particularity, i.e., seeing this from this point of view in order to accept this perspective that involves this ethical way of acting. For Wittgenstein, the importance of examining a particular way of seeing is in its connection to particular ways of acting. Thus, a service that prompts us to see the world around us in new ways carries with it the possibility of living in this world in new ways.

The disruption of the liturgical *ordo* and the shared experiences of framing and encountering texts (biblical, liturgical, communal, and personal) in new ways encourages the assembly to change our perspectives on the way that we hear Scripture, the ways that we see the world around us, and the way that we see the community and ourselves in the world. The primary goal of these encounters is to prompt us to imaginatively encounter the presence of the Divine in texts, world, and one another. Here the shared task of interpretation moves out of the hands of expert liturgical scholars who prescribe a universal liturgical *ordo* (transhistorical and transcultural) into the incarnate and embodied hands of particular communities who bring their own unique histories and experiences in hopes of sharing a glimpse of the Divine. For this to happen, the liturgy must be taken from the control of the experts in order for the assembly to have space to encounter and interpret the texts in new ways.

Similarly, the liturgical scholar recognizes that her role is not to fix the meaning(s) of liturgical text. Instead, the liturgy becomes a place of imaginary encounter with the multiple layers of the text. This imaginative engagement with the world(s) of the text is the scope of the liturgy as prepared and as embodied in order to point to places where all those who participate in the service may encounter God.

---

14. Wittgenstein, *Philosophical Investigations*, PI 144, 57e. For more on Wittgenstein's applicability to liturgical theology, see my book *Doxology and Theology: An Investigation of the Apostles' Creed in Light of Ludwig Wittgenstein* (2008).

TOWARDS ECO-LITURGICAL SUSTAINABILITY

Addressing these issues in the context of the liturgy requires continued work to be done at the variety of the levels identified by the Nairobi Statement. When the transcultural elements are given too much weight, then the other cultural elements are diminished. Here, once again, the focus turns to the local and particular. This congregation, with these unique gifts, in this particular place, strives to give body and voice to the ways that it connects to the lives of those around us and to this particular piece of the earth.

This means that spiritual-moral formation is irreducibly concrete and local, even when it is formation of a shared earth ethic. It happens person by person, congregation by congregation, institution by institution, system by system. And it happens by way of multiple points of entry and multiple means as expressed by the whole people of God—young and old, lettered and unlettered, male and female, of whatever race, class, nationality of ecclesial tradition.[15]

As an important first step, congregations need to connect to the environmental issues and needs of the land and water that is in their own communities. A distinctive feature of this form of ecological commitment by a faith community is that it is characterized by activism that is rooted in prayer. Community engagement in earth care issues is not simply the designated work of a particular committee. Instead, to care for the earth is a part of the life of discipleship of the entire congregation. In this perspective, earth care begins at the baptismal font. Here, the water we use from our neighborhood is integral to the ritual way in which we pour water over our bodies to mark ourselves as beloved children of God. In this act in which we celebrate how God's grace claims and sustains us, we gather around water and share promises with one another to live faithfully as disciples of Jesus Christ.

An important recognition of the linkage between discipleship and earth care has included an additional baptismal vow in the Anglican Church of Canada:

> Presider: "Will you strive to safeguard the integrity of God's creation, and respect, sustain and renew the life of the Earth?"
> Baptismal Candidate: "I will, with God's help."[16]

---

15. Rasmussen, "Eco-Justice," 18.
16. Hair, "Covenant and Care."

The addition of this vow provides a clear articulation that Christian faith includes a commitment to care for the goodness of God's creation. This foundation provides a starting place for both the community and individuals to build upon in terms of the ways in which we live out our baptismal promises.

A Christian commitment to earth care begins in the worshiping life of the community and grows into a central component of Christian faith. What is pictured here is not simply the addition of an annual Earth Day service or an occasional sermon on creation, but a transformation of our Christian identity in which our theological commitment to care for creation is central to the life of faith.

Regular prayer for the health and cleanliness of local lakes and rivers prompts actions to service projects that embody our faith. At a recent national conference, participants were asked to write the name of their local watershed on slips of paper. During the service, worshipers were invited to thread the slips of paper through nets that were placed at one side of the worship space. With this action, an awareness of our own watershed was connected to the worshiping life of the assembly. At the end of the conference, we were invited to remove slips of paper from the net to take with us as a sign of commitment to pray for one another as we work to address the health and well-being of our own local water resources.

From this foundation, weekly worship provides a biblical and theological vocabulary that cultivates and guides Christian engagement in the world around us. Local congregations can develop ways to build upon a theological commitment that responds to the local and particular needs of their own communities. Earth care projects are more than special programs for those who are interested, but are invitations for us to live out Christian faith in our own neighborhoods. Congregational leaders can chart a course that maps out the connections between caring for the earth and the ecological needs of their particular communities.

I have spent the past year working with a group of congregations in the Pacific Northwest by exploring ways that worship can reflect ongoing concerns and actions that relate to caring for creation. My work included drafting a series of liturgies for services during the season of Easter that were used by several congregations. The focal point of these liturgies is to discover ways that ecological concerns can explore the dynamic tension between form and freedom. Or to put it in the terms of the Nairobi Statement: How can an emphasis on liturgical contextuality as it relates to environmental concerns provide a counter voice to the emphasis on the universal dimensions of liturgical expression that can mute the expression of particular issues? While the acceptance of the critical nature of liturgical contextuality obviously takes on a myriad of local forms, the need for congregations to experiment with services is especially high when it comes to ecological issues that are inevitably expressed in local ways (e.g., as concern over the quality of *this* river).

The following worship service was crafted to address the particular needs of a local congregation to strengthen their commitment to exploring ways to connect Christian faith and ecological conservation. The service was created following a series of conservations that included: meeting with the eco-justice committee, a congregational forum on worship and ecology, and participation and leadership in Sunday morning worship services. Five years ago, two members of the congregation of First Presbyterian Church in Newport, Oregon, started a committee on eco-spirituality. The work of the committee has explored conservation issues for the church building, the use of church property for a community garden, eco-theological resources for the church library, greener resources for the church kitchen and fellowship times, and occasional worship services that highlight ecological themes. Because of this history, the recognition and commissioning of earth stewards serves as an important next step of engaging additional members from the church and from the broader community.

The service uses basic liturgical patterns that are known in the congregation, but adapts them to address particular concerns regarding caring for creation. Primary attention is given to the contextual element: Local congregations need to identify and build their own particular eco-liturgical resources as a way of recognizing local leaders and issues. Liturgical resources developed and used for the season of Easter drew from the Revised Common Lectionary readings for the day to discover imagery of nature and the earth were woven into the regular worship gatherings of congregations. A primary value is for the rich biblical imagery of the earth to reappear in worship services.

At the same time, the service draws on other areas highlighted in the Nairobi Statement: a) The transcultural with its emphasis on the role of Scripture, Table, and Water to shape the identity of Christians throughout the history of the church; b) The cross-cultural use of liturgical resources for the season of Easter drawn from the Revised Common Lectionary readings for the day to discover imagery of nature and the earth were woven into the regular worship gatherings of congregations; and c) a counter-cultural witness to the role of Christians as stewards of creation in a society that is driven by consumer approaches.

This represents one particular example of the way that attention to the contextual elements of worship can both challenge and support liturgical patterns in the life of congregations. The service disrupts the "traditional shape of the *ordo*" (gathering, word, thanksgiving, sending) by emphasizing movements for this particular occasion (word, sending, thanksgiving, gathering). Within the service itself, primary attention is paid to the recognition and commissioning of earth stewards and to encouraging ways in which their gifts and leadership skills can prompt the congregation to join them in their work of caring for creation.

CONCLUSION

It is imperative for congregations to rediscover ways to address the ecological concerns that their communities are facing. It is not enough to simply have a service for Earth Day. Instead, the church needs to reexamine our primary liturgical resources (Word and Sacrament) in order to find ongoing ways in which they connect us with our daily care for creation. Here, the church seeks to make a contribution as we work alongside other people of faith as well as people without faith.

As we have seen, the process of engaging in this work also allows the church to reexamine the balance of power outlined in the Nairobi Statement on culture. The growing awareness of addressing local, ecological concerns can provide an important counterbalance to the liturgical fixation with transcultural, transhistorical elements. Attention to the contextual elements provides a particular, incarnational focus to services that show a diversity of ways in which a liturgical *ordo* can unfold. This work also underscores the need for additional reflection on the other axis of the Nairobi Statement around the balance between the counter-cultural and the cross-cultural components. It is an invitation into services that are fluid and diverse in the ways that the gospel is proclaimed and enacted. Following is an example of the kind of service that a congregation could adapt to fit its own needs:

EASTER SUNDAY EVENING

Annotated service

Word

Service begins in community garden with turning of the soil and recognition of the land as blessed.

Scripture: 1 Cor 5:6b–8

Homily: Yeast—An Easter Experiment in Rising

Several years ago, I received approval from the Bishop of Gibraltar in Europe to preside at Eucharist in a service at the English Church in Heidelberg. The service was to be conducted under the supervision of my friend Emile, a duly ordained Anglican priest from Sierra Leone. Early one Sunday morning at the conclusion of the service, we faced a dilemma: what to do with the chalice of consecrated wine. Emile was on dialysis and it was a little early in the day for me to chug a chalice of wine, so we stood in the sacristy and pondered what we should do with the consecrated wine. After considering our options, we finally agreed to take it in to the courtyard of the church and pour it into the ground as a way of returning the wine to the earth from which it came.[17] It was only much later that I discovered that this dilemma of how to properly dispose of consecrated wine had been hotly debated and we had unknowingly chosen one of the options that was approved by at least some parts of the church.[18]

17. For example, note this discussion: "Under ordinary circumstances both the bread and the wine should be consumed. Under extraordinary circumstances, however, the consecrated elements may be buried in the ground." Diocese of Florida, "Diocesan Protocol," 4.

18. See also the document by the Churches Together in England, "Guidelines for Methods of Administration of Holy Communion and the Disposal of Remaining Eucharistic Elements":

> What is done with the remaining elements depends on what it is believed has happened to the elements, and what the context of their use is perceived to be—only for that particular Eucharist, or for extended communion, or reservation for the sick, or reservation for the purpose of devotion. In some traditions it has been the practice to treat the elements with what others would regard as disrespect, in order to make a theological point. With time, what was a theological point has become a matter of indifference, and is interpreted as casualness by those from another tradition. The deep offence that this can cause has to be recognised and must be handled generously.

This evening, we are gathering here in the garden for a service to celebrate Christ's resurrection and to recognize and to commission members of this congregation whose lives and actions model ways to care for the world that God created. We are recognizing those among us who pour out their lives in service and care of the beauty of creation. In these days of climate change and environmental pollution, we all have an urgent need to live in ways that minimize our footprint and preserve the beauty of the earth for the coming generations. Tonight, though, we recognize as guides on this journey of earth care several people whose commitment to creation care is rooted in their understanding of Christian faith and service.

Our Scripture readings this evening uses the imagery of yeast—that small miraculous form of alchemy that causes bread to rise and gives it a distinct flavor. It is an apt metaphor for the work in which we are asking you to lead us. Given the enormity of environmental crises that face us, it is easy for us to get discouraged and become complacent. This evening, as we recognize and commission earth stewards, we invite you to model for us this image of serving as yeast—that which stirs up and prepares us to create something new: this new batch that allows us to celebrate the feast of Christ's resurrection.

Sending

Commissioning of Earth Stewards

Today, we gather in this garden to recognize those whose gifts show us ways to care for the earth and to provide for our neighbors.

An ecumenical respect for the other position may well lead to some form of reverent disposal. When there is general agreement that reverent disposal is appropriate, there may still be different views on what "reverent" means. For example, some will regard it as appropriate to give bread to the birds and to pour wine into the ground, "returning the elements to nature." Others will see consumption of what remains as the most appropriate form of reverence: but elements can be consumed discreetly, out of full view of the congregation or after the service. Ecumenical generosity would suggest respecting those who find public consumption of the remaining elements unedifying or offensive (washing-up does not usually take place at a dinner table in front of the guests) and reverent disposal may be shared by the elders/deacons/assistants. *Baptism, Eucharist and Ministry* points to reverent consumption; the Church of England's *Guidelines on the Ecumenical Canons* argue that "This provision for reverent consumption dates back to the 1662 Book of Common Prayer and has helped to hold in unity worshippers with a variety of understandings of Christ's presence in the Eucharist."

Hear these words of Scripture:

> We know that the whole creation has been groaning in labor pains until now; and not only the creation, but we ourselves, who have the first fruits of the Spirit, groan inwardly while we wait for adoption, the redemption of our bodies. For in hope we were saved. (Rom 8:22–24)

In our baptism, "we are called by God to be the church of Jesus Christ, A sign in the world today of what God intends for all humankind."19

N. and N., as a way to live out your baptismal promises,

Will you care for the goodness of creation and show us ways to preserve the signs of God's presence among us?

Will you live out your call to discipleship in ways that welcome others to join you in this ministry?

Laying on of Hands: All are invited to lay hands on those being commissioned as a sign of blessing.20

> Creating God, pour out your Spirit
> On these whose ministry
> Leads us in ways to see
> The goodness of your creation
> And to care for the world around us.
> Give them strength to work for the renewal
> That you are bringing to the earth.
> Guide them to discover ways to invite all people
> Into finding your presence in the world around us
> And responding by caring for creation.
> We ask this in the name of Jesus Christ,
> The firstborn of creation. Amen.

"Whatever you do, in word or deed, do everything in the name of the Lord Jesus, giving thanks to God through him" (Col 3:7).

---

19. Presbyterian Church (U.S.A.), "Commissioning to Ministry Outside a Congregation," 130. Language for commissioning both within and outside the congregation is identical.

20. This action seeks to challenge the pattern of allowing only ministers and elders to participate in the act of laying on of hands in the ordination rites.

Part Three: The Earth as Guide for Our Future

Passing of the Peace

Procession into Fellowship Hall

Water that has been collected outside is carried inside.

Thanksgiving

Eucharist/Agape Meal

Easter Eucharistic Prayer

Invitation to the Table

Hear these words of Scripture:

> Behold, I stand at the door and knock
> If those who hear my voice open the door,
> I will come in and eat with them
> And they with me.

At this table, all are welcome.
The Lord be with you.

And also with you.

Lift up your hearts.

We lift them up to the Lord.

Let us give thanks to God.

It is good to give our thanks and praise.

God, we give you thanks that
In the beginning, you created heaven and earth:
Plants, animals, and humans
And you declared that all creation was good.
When we turned away from you and plundered
    the richness of the earth
You continued to call out to us
Through the beauty of the earth
And through prophets that spoke of your mercy and grace.

In the fullness of time, you sent Jesus who taught us to look
        for your presence
In the lilies of the field and the sparrows in the trees.
So we join our voices in praising you with the birds that sing
and with all creation that calls out to you:

> **Holy, holy, holy Lord**
> **God of power and might**
> **Heaven and earth are full of your glory**
> **Hosanna in the highest.**
> **Blessed is the one who comes in the name of the Lord**
> **Hosanna in the highest.**

We speak of your holiness and we give thanks for our brother Jesus
who showed us the way to work for peace and justice for our world.
In his life, baptism, teaching, death, and resurrection,
We discover your redeeming presence that continues to bring forth
        new life.
We take this bread made from the grain that grows up out
        of the earth
And this juice/wine made from grapes that flourish in the sun
and declare your steadfast love that claims us as your beloved sons and
        daughters.
We offer you our lives that we may become signs of your grace in our
        world.
Great is the mystery of faith:

> **Christ has died.**
> **Christ is risen.**
> **Christ will come again.**

Send your Spirit upon us and upon this bread and this cup
That we may be able to see your presence in these gifts of creation,
in the world around us, in our neighbors, and in our own lives.
Send us out into the world that we may work for the coming
        of your reign.
Help us feed the hungry,
Welcome the stranger,
Clothe the naked,
Care for the sick,
Visit those imprisoned,

And discover your presence with them.
Fill us with hope
So that we may share in the resurrection life that you bring
    to our world.
Unite us in Christ by the power of your Spirit as we offer
    our thanksgiving to you
the Creator and Sustainer of all.

Amen.

The Lord's Prayer

Breaking of the Bread

When Jesus was at table with his disciples
He took the bread and blessed it
Broke it and gave it to them
And their eyes were opened and they recognized him.
The disciples turned to one another and said,

Were not our hearts burning within us
When the Scriptures were opened to us?[21]

Brothers and Sisters in Christ:
Look and taste
At this table
God's gifts are offered to all.

Testimony of Earth Stewards and Table Conversation

Each earth steward will come to the table and take a loaf of bread and a bottle of wine to each table.

At each table the steward will share the bread and wine with all at the table.

---

21. For eucharistic prayers that do not include the words of institution, note the 2001 decision by the Vatican that recognized the practices of the Assyrian Church. See Taft, "Mass Without the Consecration?"

The earth steward will speak briefly of how she/he has encountered God in nature and invite those around the table to speak of places and occasions when they have encountered God.

People are invited to bring pictures of places where they have encountered God.

Pictures and lists of the places that people mention at the tables will be collected by the earth stewards and brought to the sanctuary to be placed near the baptismal font.

Gathering

Procession to Sanctuary—Gathered around the font for blessing of one another

Pictures and lists placed around baptismal space

Pour water into font—

We have been blessed in these places where we have encountered God and together we will work to care for the earth so that it may continue to be a sign of God's goodness to all people.

Congregational members are invited to dip their hands into the water and offer prayers of blessings for one another and for the earth.

Service ends by taking water from the font back to the garden and pouring it into the ground that has been turned. Commissioned earth stewards will take water from the font and lead the assembly back to the garden to return the water to the earth and offer a blessing of the community garden.

As we leave this garden, I offer you the words of the Russian novelist Fyodor Dostoyevsky:

> Love all of God's creation, the whole of it and every grain of sand. Love every leaf, every ray of God's light! Love the animals, love the plants, love everything. If you love everything, you will perceive the divine mystery in things. Once you perceive it, you will begin to comprehend it better every day. And you will come at last to love the whole world with an all-embracing love.[22]

22. Dostoyevsky, *Brothers Karamazov*, 167.

10

The Search for Earth-Inclusive Language

A Brief Exploration of Three New Prayers in the Revised *Book of Common Worship*

INTRODUCTION

IN LIGHT OF THE ecological crisis that we currently are facing, congregations are finally raising questions and trying out possible responses for ways to engage in earth care from the standpoint of Christian faith. As we have seen in previous chapters, this requires an evaluation of the church's language, theology, and practices that have distanced us from the earth. Included in this work is the development of new liturgical resources that show the connection between faith and creation care. In this chapter, we will examine portions of the newest worship book of the Presbyterian Church (U.S.A.) that particularly correspond to the intersection between ecology and worship.

For Reformed communities, the task of liturgical revision and renewal has been guided by a theological commitment to the role of biblical warrants in terms of providing liturgical resources. From this perspective, Scripture itself provides both a normative guide and faithful language that orients communities as they gather to worship. This guiding principle grew out of the critiques of liturgical practices during the Protestant Reformation and continues to serve in a distinctive way both in terms of providing a critical assessment of worship language and practices of other Christian communities as well as providing a biblical basis for the development of new liturgical resources.[1] Given this commitment, one might expect Reformed liturgies to build on the central role of the earth throughout Scripture. Calvin offers a deep appreciation of the beauty of creation as witness to God's presence and in his typical form of theological argument includes biblical citations that support his case.

> . . . wherever you cast your eyes, there is no spot in the universe wherein you cannot discern at least some sparks of his [God's] glory. You cannot in one glance survey this most vast and beautiful system of the universe, in its wide expanse, without being completely overwhelmed by the boundless force of its brightness. The reason why the author of The Letter to the Hebrews elegantly calls the universe the appearance of things invisible [Heb 11:3] is that this skillful ordering of the universe is for us a sort of mirror in which we can contemplate God, who is otherwise invisible. The reason why the prophet attributes to the heavenly creatures a language known to every nation [Ps 19:2 ff.] is that therein lies an attestation of divinity so apparent that it ought not to escape the gaze of even the most stupid tribe.[2]

For Calvin, though, this clear witness of God's presence in the world around us is not to be identified as or confused with "saving knowledge" since humans are blinded by sin and unable to see the clear signs that surround us. It is only through the witness of Scripture that we are able to clearly come to the knowledge of God as Creator and source of our salvation (see *Institutes*, 1.VI).

This tension within Calvin has often been overlooked by his interpreters. A preference for strictly spiritual (versus material) categories and language took hold in ways that seemed to eliminate possibilities to speak of God's presence and revelation in the world around us. Reformed communities have subsequently been challenged in regards to a positive appropriation of earth language due to the theological resistance and suspicion of language that might imply any acceptance or endorsement of natural theology.

This issue rose again to the forefront in Karl Barth's famous rebuttal of Emil Brunner's theology in "Nein! Antwort an Emil Brunner" in 1934.

---

1. Note how the *BCW* itself documents this principle by providing biblical references for each movement in the liturgy.

2. Calvin, *Institutes* 1.5.1, 52–53.

Barth rejected any form of natural theology as incompatible with a theology centered solely on the revelation known in Jesus Christ. Barth's declaration and opposition to all forms of general revelation provided additional support for those within the Reformed tradition who were hesitant to include language, images, objects, and actions that suggested God's presence in any way in the "matter" of this world. To cite but one example, note Kim Dorr's concluding analysis of Barth's insistence that special revelation served as the only possible source for theology and liturgy: any alternative approach risked making matter into a source of idolatry: "Outside of revelation, working only with the tangible stuff of this world, the outcome, as Barth understood it, is that humanity is deified while God Almighty is humanized and God comes to exist primarily as an idea which merely services humanity's exaltation."[3]

A growing reassessment of the heightened, historical contextuality of Barth's argument against all forms of general revelation includes Barth's own communication to Brunner near the time of Brunner's death in 1966 when Barth communicated that "the time when I thought I should say No to him is long since past."[4] More recently, Alister McGrath's reassessment of Brunner's theology suggests important ways that Barth distorted Brunner's position on general revelation.[5]

At long last, it seems that the time is ripe for Reformed communities to look again at the theological presuppositions that have led us to seeing ourselves apart from the world around us. As we have seen, this theological reassessment includes a reappropriation of Calvin's deep appreciation of God's witness in creation and a rediscovery of the ways that Scripture itself acknowledges, testifies, and witnesses to the central role of creation as a source for people of faith. To this end, now is the time for the church's liturgy and witness to give full voice to the sounds of praise and laments of the earth.

3. Dorr, "Karl Barth." For a similar conclusion, see Grow, "No Theology Proper."

4. From Barth's letter to Peter Vogelsanger in 1966 that was read to Brunner shortly before his death. Barth, "Letter 207."

5. See McGrath, *Emil Brunner*.

THE TASK OF REVISING THE BOOK
OF COMMON WORSHIP

For Presbyterians, the 1993 publication of the *Book of Common Worship* represented a defining moment in terms of embracing the results of the liturgical renewal movement. The production of the book reaped the benefits of revisions to other mainline Protestant worship books that were published before it. In many ways, the book represented the lifelong project of liturgical scholar and longtime North American Academy of Liturgy member Harold Daniels. The book was recognized by many in the ecumenical community as a significant liturgical contribution not simply for those in the Reformed community, but for the ecumenical church as well.

In advance of the twenty-fifth anniversary of the publication of the BCW, the Office of Theology and Worship of the Presbyterian Church (U.S.A.) decided to produce a revised edition of the worship book. While the publication of the new edition in 2018 seeks to preserve the body of work that was originally published, Kimberly Long, who served as one of the editors of the project, alludes to a couple of priorities in the revised edition that include a more sustained attention both to baptismal language and to creation care.[6]

The process of revising the book was primarily done by consultation and online collaboration (with working groups in particular areas such as eucharistic prayer, creation care, etc.). As one of the participants in the creation care group, I can report that there was significant discussion about how to best achieve the goals of the group. While we recognized the need to provide resources particularly oriented to ecological concerns (which has resulted, for example, in a section of prayers on occasions of natural disaster), there was a strong preference that earth oriented language not be confined to one section of a revised worship book, but that eco-centric liturgical language needed to be incorporated throughout the book.

A second tendency emerged during the initial submission of materials for the creation care section of the book: a proclivity to use earth language as a spiritual metaphor for a deeper truth (and thereby ironically discount the role of the earth). Let me illustrate with two examples of the way that this process has happened previously in terms of the appropriation of biblical texts about the earth.

---

6. Long, "A New Worship Book."

1. The Psalter in the BCW

One of the contributions of the 1993 edition of the BCW was to include a Psalter. The Psalter was an attempt to reinvigorate the historic practice of sung psalms that was central to the worship practices of early Reformed communities, such as St. Pierre in Geneva where John Calvin served as pastor. Accompanying this edition of the Psalms was a collection of Psalm prayers (from a variety of resources) that were part of the tradition of the Church of Scotland. Notice though the way that the Psalm prayer in the 1993 BCW frames and interprets Psalm 98.

> O sing to the Lord a new song,
> > for he has done marvelous things.
> **The right hand and the holy arm of the Lord**
> > **have secured the victory.**
> The Lord has made known this victory;
> > and has openly showed righteousness in the sight of the nations.
> **The Lord remembers mercy and faithfulness to the house of Israel and**
> > **all the ends of the earth have seen the victory of our God.**
> Shout with joy to the Lord, all you lands,
> > lift up your voice, rejoice, and sing.
> **Sing praises to the Lord with the harp,**
> > **with the harp and the voice of song.**
> With trumpets and the sound of the horn
> > make a joyful noise before the Sovereign, the Lord.
> **Let the sea roar, and all that fills it;**
> > **the world and those who live in it.**
> Let the rivers clap their hands,
> > and let the hills ring out with joy before the Lord,
> > who is coming to judge the earth.
> **In righteousness shall the Lord judge the world**
> > **and the peoples with equity.**

> *Psalm Prayer:*
> Eternal God, You redeemed humanity by sending your only Son in fulfillment of your promises of old. Let the truth and power of your salvation be known in all places of the earth, that all nations may give you praise, honor, and glory; through Jesus Christ your Son. Amen.

Instead of an invitation to join with creation in its praise of God, the Psalm prayer provides a hermeneutical lens that points in a different direction. The doxological references that are at the center of this psalm are completely minimized by the way the prayer chooses to point instead to the earth as a place of soteriological possibility.

A second place to note the tendency to spiritualize the prominent role of the earth in Scripture is to observe the way that the earth is frequently treated in sermons. For example, note the way that the Jordan River often is portrayed in sermons on 2 Kings 5. Frequently when theologians read this famous text about the healing of Naaman, we take our cue from the mention of the Jordan River. The Jordan River is the famous place where Joshua and the Hebrews crossed as they made their way into the promised land flowing with milk and honey. It is the same river where John the Baptist preached and where Jesus joined the throngs of people who were baptized as an act of preparation for the coming of the kingdom of God. More often than not, by the end of the sermon the Jordan River is not so much a body of water as it is an idea that we use to support our own particular theological cause. Rather than actually reflect on the role of water in this story, we often end up in some dry theoretical landscape.

Here, once again, an eco-centric approach to homiletics and liturgics will insist on taking the earth seriously as a resource in itself and a place of encountering the glory of God and not simply as a metaphor for an implicitly gnostic spirituality that uses earth language in order to foster its own theological goals. It is time for Reformed Christians in particular to reclaim Calvin's language of the earth as the theater of God's glory and witness. The recovery of earth language and images reasserts a central Christian belief and experience of God's presence in our daily lives and in the world around us.

EMBRACING THE EARTH: THREE LITURGICAL EXAMPLES

How can we begin to listen to the biblical texts and to the witness of the creation in order to recover a central place for the earth in our worshiping assemblies? What follows are three particular examples from the liturgy that reflect a renewed commitment to earth language from the revised BCW.

1. Confession and Pardon

The role of confession and pardon is central to Reformed worship. Typically, the placement of confession and pardon comes early in the service as a response to the opening call to worship and hymn of praise. The theological rationale for the placement in the liturgy is that we are called to worship in order to praise God's greatness and in response to this awareness we recognize our own failings and shortcomings. Thus, the role of confession and pardon is in response to an emphasis on God's faithfulness and mercy. The corporate nature of this prayer stresses the ways that we as a community and as individuals have failed to love God and care for our neighbor.

A renewed attention to the human contributions to climate change, pollutions, and environmental degradation as well as a sustained commitment to the role of humans in caring for the earth invite us to expand our language in ways that make clear the role and responsibilities that we as humans have in responding to environmental challenges and to caring for the earth as central to our baptismal identities as beloved children of God. The following confession seeks to take these issues seriously by extending our confession to include our role in harming and ignoring the plight of the earth as well as articulating the way that the earth itself displays the Creator's presence.

Example One: Prayer of Confession

God of light and life, You created us in your image to care for one another and for all of creation. Forgive us for turning away from you, embracing the darkness, and ignoring the needs of our neighbor and the cries of the earth. Help us to see your presence in all life and creation. As the sun brings light and warmth to this earth, make us signs of your grace, through Christ, our light and life, we pray. Amen.

Assurance of Pardon

In the water of baptism, God's blessing is poured out upon us. All creation declares the goodness of God. May the light of Christ shine in our lives so that all may see God's glory. May the Spirit's blessing lead us to share in creation's song of glory.

As additional new prayers of confession that contain earth language are included in our liturgies, it will be important that these prayers reflect a full range of images and seasons of nature. Our prayers should include the ways in which light and darkness both provide balance and opportunity for growth. Our prayers should allude to the seasons of nature and the seasons of our own lives. Our prayers should reference times of rapid growth and times of dying and rising again. The recovery of eco-centric language in our prayers offers us ways to integrate our experiences with the world as an integral part of our spirituality.

2. Blessing and Charge

A second element of the liturgy that we will examine is the blessing and charge at the end of the service. The primary role of the blessing and charge is to encourage the assembly to live out their baptismal call to love God and care for neighbor and creation as part of their commitment to discipleship (note the possibilities for connecting this with the language of the Confession and Pardon). I believe that the common language of "sending" that is often employed in this section of the service has reinforced the tendency for us to see worship as a place that is somehow distinct from the world around us. In this approach, the language of gathering and sending imply a degree of separation that requires us to be sent back into the world. Such a perspective often carries with it a notion that we have something to take with us or a task to do that will somehow fix the problems that the world faces. The inclusion of eco-centric language can help us reframe this element of the liturgy so that we avoid the dangers of reinforcing understandings of spirituality that support privatistic and individualistic notions of faith by showing our deeper connections with the world around us. A renewed eco-centric liturgy eschews anthropocentric understandings of Christian faith and life and points to the deeper interconnections between all forms of life.

Example Two: Blessing and Charge

> *Go and join the song of creation that sings out in praise to God.*
> *Go and join the cries of creation that sighs and yearns for healing.*
> *Go and work for healing and wholeness of all the earth.*
> *May the One who creates us, go with and before us,*
> *May the One who saves us, lead us into everlasting life,*
> *May the One who gives us wisdom, guide us in the way of peace.*
> *Amen.*

In this example, the blessing and charge invite and urge the assembly to more fully participate in the ongoing work of creation and redemption that God is doing in the world.

3. Baptismal Prayer

As we have seen in the first two examples, the revisions to the BCW seek to address two primary concerns that are connected as related concerns: earth care and baptismal living. In each of these instances, the recovery of language of the earth is placed alongside a call to respond with the earth and to the earth as an integral part of our baptismal identity and life of discipleship. Such an approach can only make theological sense if our baptismal rites themselves reflect these priorities. Simply recovering biblical and theological images and language of creation in parts of our liturgies will not create a coherent portrait of Christian life that reflects our role and responsibilities as part of God's creation. New baptismal rites must be rooted in a deeper baptismal theology that points to sustained ways in which a baptismal life of discipleship makes radical claims on our priorities and lives.

The limitations of current baptismal rites have been underscored by feminist critiques of ways that the ritual and its language marginalized and supplanted the role of women in favor of asserting patriarchal authority. I want to point broadly to three significant aspects of this critique.

First, the historical dominance and authority of male leadership has usurped the role of women and failed to recognize their central role as those who give birth. An initial critique by feminists is that the baptismal liturgy erases and supplants the physical act of birth by women in favor of a rite that places men in the role of those who initiate the spiritual (and more important) birth of a child. Theologian Susan Ross observes the way that this often takes form within the institutional church: "Women give physical birth, but spiritual birth—'real' birth—is given by male clerics in baptism."[7] This concern points to the highly patriarchal tradition of the church through which the role of women has been perpetually diminished not only in terms of leadership roles, but more broadly in terms of supplanting the role of women to bring forth and nurture life by defining and using rituals as ways to marginalize and exclude the voices and experiences of women. As Christine Gudorf summarizes, "the exclusion of women from sacred rituals is based in a fear of their power over life, and that this power over life is so central that men ritually claim it for themselves."[8]

---

7. Ross, *Extravagant Affections*, 193.
8. Gudorf in Ross, *Extravagant Affections*, 193.

Second, in communities of faith that have (finally) ordained women to serve in roles that fully allow them to preside as sacramental leaders, the language of the rite continues to perpetuate the church's position of ignoring the gift of physical birth that is undertaken by birth mothers (often at the risk of their own lives) in favor of the celebration of new birth that is provided by the rites and under the auspices of the church (usually in language that is primarily, if not exclusively, masculine). While advocating for the ordination of women and for the use of inclusive language in our liturgies is essential, there remain other layers of the rite that need sustained attention. The language of baptismal rites (for infants) simply must make room to acknowledge the act of physical birth and women's role in this life-giving process as the community gathers and celebrates around the baptismal font.

Third, more recently, other voices have raised concerns about baptismal rites and practices that use minimal amounts of water with limited references to the earth and creation. For example, the current BCW offers two Prayers of Thanksgiving over the water as part of the baptismal rite. One of the two prayers includes a brief mention of the connection between water and creation, but fails to follow up with any other references to the earth.[9]

Aside from this brief reference point, the longer baptismal prayers with their lack of references to the world around us reinforces the tendency to see this primarily as a spiritual event and serves to reinforce the interpretations of this event as individualistic and responding to the requests and needs of "consumers" (those who are requesting baptism for themselves or their children for whatever felt need they may hold). Attempts to address aspects of this problem have included attention to the ways that the baptismal rite has often been reduced. These are two frequent examples: 1) to note the decrease of water that is used in the rite itself (with baptismal fonts holding smaller amounts of water and presiders using less water in the baptism itself); or 2) to observe the truncation or privatization of the rite (external to the central worshiping assembly as a private or separate rite).

These significant and well-intentioned critiques of current baptismal practice have insisted on the need for ample amounts of water and the return of the baptismal rite to Sunday worship. While these are important correctives on the way to a more robust baptismal theology, on their own, they are insufficient steps to address the deeper problems of our baptismal

---

9. "We give you thanks, Eternal God, for you nourish and sustain all living things by the gift of water." Presbyterian Church (U.S.A.), *Book of Common Worship*, 410.

theology. More water and longer rites alone will not reorient us to the biblical witness of the centrality of the earth and the theo-ethical dimensions and demands of discipleship that include caring for the earth. These actions require a renewed commitment to an eco-centric language in our baptismal liturgies that offers a clearly incarnational grounding of Christian life and faith. These liturgies take their cue from ethicist Larry Rasmussen's call for religious communities to reclaim their sacramental center: "The basic ethical reorientation commended here belongs to an eco-spirituality that includes a profoundly sacramental sense. Water is the object of awe and not *only* the object of engineering; it is the medium of the mystical and not *only* a resource for a world of our own making; water is a 'thou' and not *only* an 'it.'"[10]

New baptismal rites will build on this understanding by advocating for increased attention to earth imagery and language and through underscoring the ways in which baptism represents our immersion into the world rather than our separation from it. In this way, new baptismal rites seek to balance long-standing theological emphases of the church's baptismal practice and language with the biblical and historic witness of God's participation in creation and new creation. This new commitment to an eco-sacramental understanding builds on the testimony of early church fathers like Melito of Sardis who connected Jesus' baptism in the Jordan River with a "universal baptismal liturgy." As theologian Linda Gibler notes, "For Melito baptism in water is an ongoing process in which all of creation naturally participates. . . . Jesus was baptized in water because everything is baptized in water."[11] This approach to baptismal liturgy and practice immerses us in a renewed vision of the earth as a place of discovery and encounter with the Divine.

Example Three: Prayer of Thanksgiving Over the Water/Baptismal Prayer

> *In the beginning, when your Spirit moved over the face of the waters,*
>   *light and life emerged from the dark and formless void.*
> *At your calling, all creation came forth and you declared that it was good.*
> *Within the presence of the same Spirit of light and life,*
>   *we give thanks for the gift of water that sustains life:*

10. Rasmussen, *Earth-Honoring Faith*, 282.
11. Gibler, *From the Beginning to Baptism*, 24.

For the earth and the air
  for plants and trees,
  for birds and fish,
  for animals and humans.
In the gift of your covenant, you led your people
  through the Red Sea and out of slavery to freedom.
By the rivers of Babylon, you offered consolation to your people in captivity.
When Jesus was baptized in the Jordan River,
  all creation was blessed by you.
Through his death on the cross, Jesus' baptism became complete
  and in his resurrection the gift of eternal life is available to all.
We gather around this water to give thanks for the gift of birth
  and for the experience of new birth.
We receive this water as part of the earth that you created,
  *[from the local rivers of *** (at this point the celebrant will name the lo-*
  cal rivers near the gathering)]
  and pour it over our bodies to mark us as followers of Jesus Christ,
  and to celebrate our calling as beloved children of God.
We give thanks for N. whose call to discipleship we celebrate in the sacra-
  ment of baptism.
By your Spirit, breathe new life upon the one who passes through this water.
Bind them to your unending love and to the community of faith
  that they may share with joy this life of discipleship and mission, serving
  all in need.
Give them strength to follow faithfully in the way of Christ
  that they may serve as a sign of your redemptive love
  by caring for others and for the world that you created.
We praise you and thank you for your goodness that creates us,
  calls us, and claims us as your own beloved children.
To you, Holy One, Holy Three, be all glory and honor. Amen.

This baptismal prayer draws insights from feminist critiques by beginning the long task of reclaiming the gift of birth as central to this celebration. In addition, this example shows an important way that the language of a baptismal rite can connect biblical stories of creation with the call to see God's presence in the world around us and to commit to caring for it as central to our lives of discipleship.

CONCLUSION: TOWARDS A SUSTAINED, ECO-CENTRIC, LITURGICAL VISION OF CHRISTIAN LIFE

These three examples show ways that particular prayers in the *Book of Common Worship* seek to integrate earth care as a central part of Christian faith. Each of these liturgical occasions seeks to challenge ways in which patterns of Christian living have lacked connection with the earth. Three central liturgical moments of confessing, blessing/sending, and baptizing are reconfigured by the theological conviction that caring for the earth is basic to our lives as followers of Jesus Christ. Other resources in the BCW share similar commitments. Generally, one can see evidence of a growing awareness of the need to correct the way in which liturgical language has often avoided acknowledging both the earth and our bodies. There are moments throughout this new worship book where the incarnational language of creation begins to make headway into our theological language. Especially noteworthy are the ways that the prayers of thanksgiving and intercession that are a part of the daily prayer services include petitions each morning for those engaged in caring for the earth and thanksgiving each evening for the goodness of creation. An extended section on creation and ecology provides a wide range of liturgical materials for services that include the blessings of animals as well as for services in response to natural disasters. Included are a selection of scriptural readings and liturgical texts that relate to care for creation.

While there is much to celebrate in this revision, it is important to note that many pastors and congregations will choose to navigate their way through the book and undergird a theology that perpetuates an escape from the earth rather than an engagement with the earth. In fact, the recommended Service for the Lord's Day that provides a basic template for Sunday worship shows little movement toward ecological awareness. Particularly, in terms of the celebration of the sacraments, the book provides dramatically different options. Of the sixteen additional prayers of great thanksgiving for use in communion, two are noteworthy in terms of their use of earth images throughout the prayer. Similarly, only one of the six baptismal prayers inserts the language of the earth throughout the prayer.

The question, then, is whether this revised book of services should be seen as marking the beginning of a new commitment to earth care. If we are to judge this as a first step along the path of dramatic change that is necessary for both our faith communities, our planet, and ourselves, then certainly it is a step in the right direction. On the other hand, in a denomination that revises its worship book every twenty to thirty years, history may well judge this effort as woefully insignificant especially in failing to provide a clearer theological voice and commitment to ways in which communal worship must come to terms with the ecological crisis that we are facing.

What we have seen is that liturgical revisions that strive to reclaim the centrality of the earth cannot be done piecemeal by adding an occasional reference to a biblical text about the earth or by an infrequent allusion to the world out there beyond our sanctuaries and church buildings. In this time of environmental crisis, what is required is a sustained attention to our liturgies and rites that reclaims the central role of the earth in the biblical witness and reframes our call to discipleship in ways that include our commitment to care for God's creation. It is imperative for us to show ways that earth care is integrally linked to the celebration of the sacraments. In fact, it is an integral part of our discipleship as those who live in light of the witness of Scripture to God's faithful presence in and around us. As we gather around the stuff of creation—of water, of grain, of grape—in the hope of Christ's presence in our midst, these gifts of the earth itself prompt us to see, speak, and act in ways that demonstrate how Christian discipleship includes reverence and care for the earth.

In the end, worship books will not save us; their words serve us well when they point towards the living Christ who continues to call us to come and follow him. There are prayers and liturgical resources within this revised worship book that can help us in the hard work of re-forming our liturgies and reclaiming our relationship with one another and our connections to the earth, the dust from which we came and to which we will return.

In these days that we are granted to live on this good earth there is a chance for us by the grace of God to create worship that is pleasing and acceptable—present ourselves, our bodies as a living offering, which is our reasonable duty (Romans 12:1). When we follow the Sprit's call, our prayers and worship point us towards a vision of a new heaven and earth where all living creatures will be saved. This is the liturgy that we seek to re-form and celebrate; one that by the Spirit brings us new ways of life that dare to speak of God and work for the common good.

Postscript

The Water We Need

2 Kings 5:1–14

USUALLY WHEN THEOLOGIANS READ this famous text about the healing of Naaman, we take our cue from the mention of the Jordan River. It's the famous river that Joshua and the Hebrews crossed as they made their way into the promised land flowing with milk and honey. It's the same river where John the Baptist preached and where Jesus joined the throngs of people who were baptized as an act of preparation for the coming of the kingdom of God. More often than not, by the end of the sermon the Jordan River is not so much a body of water as it is an idea that we use to support our own particular theological cause. Rather than actually reflect on the role of water in this story, we often end up in some dry theoretical landscape searching for an obscure meaning.

I want to point our attention to this text in a different direction. The healing in the story is presented as a surprise to Naaman on two accounts: First, he expects that Elisha, the man of God, will wave his hand or perform some form of magic trick that will cause his disease to vanish. Second, he at least wants a better option for bathing—his favorite rivers are far away and they are cleaner and more to his liking.

Here is where the twist in the story comes: The water Naaman needs for healing is nearby. It's the local river that provides a place for cleansing if only Naaman will plunge into the water. New life awaits him as long as he stops expecting someone else or some place else to do the work for him. New hope is coming his way if he can get over the expectation that the water somewhere else has special properties.

As we gather here above the Columbia River to reflect on the role of water in our lives—on how we can address the challenges that our planet faces—let me point out a couple of key insights from this story from long ago. When we put ourselves in Naaman's place, then we can begin to see similar ways that we often expect change and healing to come to our lives and to that of our planet. If only we had the right leaders . . . Or if only science would come up with a way to suddenly stop climate change . . . Or if only the solution to our challenges would be as simple as waving a wand and having everything resolved. But perhaps like Naaman, the healing that we long for and the healing that is needed starts at the banks of the water that is closest to us. It starts by turning our attention to our local streams, ponds, and lakes.

What we are facing is not just an ecological crisis. We are facing a spiritual crisis that cries out for us to reconnect with the water near our homes. I live in Asheville, North Carolina, where the French Broad River runs through the town that provides us with water, habitat, transportation, sanitation, brewing, and recreation that are essential to our way of life. It's this local water that is basic to our health and well-being. And it is this same local water that is the source for our rituals and religious celebrations.

Ethicist John Hart connects the availability of accessible, unpolluted water in the world with the ability of baptismal water to evoke images of cleansing and new life. Polluted and privatized water diminishes the power of the ritual to embody God's generosity and graciousness. The image of living water, clean and available to all, conveys God's goodness and provision in creating a world that sustains life. Hart concludes,

> Throughout the world today . . . environmental degradation and water privatization have caused water to lose its nature and role as *living water*, as a bountiful source of benefits for the common good. Water is losing also its ability to be a *sacramental* symbol, a sign in nature of God the Creator.[1]

Water does not belong to the church. We use it, but it is not ours; it is an essential element of God's creation. This evening, we used water to renew our baptismal vows as a way of acknowledging our dependence on

---

1. Hart, *Sacramental Commons*, 91.

God. As Christians, we care about the quality of water in the world around us not only because of its importance in our daily lives, but also because it is the water that runs down our foreheads in our baptisms that claims us as beloved children of God and physically connects us with the deep truth that our healing depends on our connection to the good earth that God creates and sustains.

The story of Naaman's healing in the nearby water of the Jordan River reminds us that the source of our healing comes from unlikely places that we often overlook. Remember the rivers, streams, and watersheds closest to our homes as sources for healing, wholeness, and identity.

> Holy is the night. Holy is your grace.
> Holy is your presence. Holy is this place.[2]

As we remember and give thanks for our baptisms, let us pledge to work together to protect the waters that are the source of our life and the sign of our calling as beloved children of God. To God be the glory. Amen.

---

2. Lyrics by Jim Strathdee, "Holy is the Night," on *Miracle of Dawn*, 2017.

Looking for Glory
Isaiah 6:1–8

RECENTLY, MANY OF US gathered to watch a rare solar eclipse. In Asheville, where I live, we were just outside the total eclipse zone, near 99 percent, but not quite complete. We were close enough to the desired area that additional hordes of tourists descended upon the city in advance of the great event. Our household celebrated the occurrence in a subdued fashion by making pinhole boxes for viewing. Although afternoon clouds started building and obscured part of our view, nevertheless the three generations of us living in our house loved watching the shadow shapes filter through the trees in our yard. One of the things that particularly struck me was the endless commentary on television that reported not only on the revelry of those gathered to watch the eclipse, but in particular on the spirituality of the occasion. Suddenly, broadcasters were left trying to dust off their meager theological vocabulary.

This experience has left me pondering the significance of the eclipse as an insight into our nation's psyche. What does it say that so many of our friends and neighbors who have little inclination to talk about faith or religion, suddenly find an eclipse as an occasion to speak about mystery and awe? How does the beauty and drama of an eclipse relate to the choices that we make about how we live our lives? What do we have to offer our neighbors about the ways that we look at the world around us and see the work of a Creator?

I started thinking about Scripture and especially familiar passages about the beauty of the earth—creation stories and Psalms about the beauty of the earth. Then, I found myself humming the familiar words of the

Sanctus, the song that is part of the prayer that many of us sing when we gather to celebrate the Lord's Supper:

> Holy, holy, holy Lord. God of power and might
> Heaven and earth are full of your glory
> Hosanna in the highest.
> Blessed is the One who comes in the name of the Lord.
> Hosanna in the highest.

This ancient communion hymn goes back to the fifth century. The song uses words from Isaiah 6 alongside the cries of acclamation by the palm-branch-waving crowd that greets Jesus' entry into Jerusalem described in Matthew 21. Here, Isaiah's vision and call meets with the crowd's joyful response to Jesus' triumphant entry.

What really caught my eye, though, is the way that we have adapted the Isaiah text. In Isaiah's vision, the angels declare that *the whole earth* is full of God's glory. Notice the subtle shift away from earth language in our song. No longer is it just the earth that is full of God's glory. Why is it that our song around this table where we gather around the grain and fruit from the earth points us to look up to the sky? I believe that it is indicative of a broader theological shift from focusing on the earth to pointing up to the sky. The church (and especially Reformed people) has been reluctant to embrace the earth as the place where God's presence and glory is available for us to see, encounter, and experience.

Theologian Serene Jones offers an important commentary on Calvin's description of creation as "the theater of God's glory." She notes, "Creation is not only a theater but the dwelling place of our lives: it is the vast and open space but also contained space in which we exist, the home in which our lives unfold, the world in which we move. It is also the space in which God dwells with us and we, with God."[1]

The earth as dwelling place, as place of encounter with the divine—it is this place, our home, for which we commit to care. Here we vow to respond to the daily opportunities to see, tend, nurture, and care for the earth as the place where we encounter God's glory. Here we dare to extend the words of Jesus (from Luke 4:18) to include all the wounds of the earth:

"The Spirit of the Lord is upon us, because she has anointed us to bring good news to the poor. She has sent us to proclaim release to the captives

1. Jones, "Glorious Creation, Beautiful Law," 26.

and recovery of sight to the blind, to let the oppressed go free, to proclaim the year of the Lord's favor" to participate in the healing of all creation.

One of the gifts of life is the chance to stop, look, and contemplate the beauty of God's presence in the world around us. Here, we take time to see the glory of the earth. Here, we shout our hosannas as a blessing for God's presence among us. Here, we live into our promises to serve as stewards of the earth so that we may join in the host of witnesses that declare that the whole earth is filled with God's glory.

As we take in the beauty of the towering trees and the mighty Columbia River as it carves its way through the gorge, may our bodies be filled with hosannas that we cry out in thanksgiving to God's presence. At the same time, as we witness the scars of the Eagle Creek fire, the growing threat of pollution and development to clean water and habitat, may we rise up to fight to preserve the earth as sacred space so that all may encounter the presence of the Divine in our midst.

As we pray for healing for ourselves and for the earth, we also renew our commitment to step forward and tend the earth as the place in which we encounter God's presence. How will you add your voice to the holy song of praise that rises up from the wolves? This evening, we are asking you to write down one thing on a piece of paper that you are willing to do in the coming weeks to care for the earth. As you write, may the sound of creation in the howling of the wolves prompt us to offer our own songs of praise.

Parting Words

Ephesians 5:1–8

THE BOOK OF EPHESIANS offers us two guiding images to take with us on our journey from this special place. First, live as children of the light. During this week together, we have renewed our baptismal vows and our commitment to care for the earth and one another. In these challenging times, where it feels like darkness is rapidly encroaching into our lives, it is important for us to take this image to heart. To live as children of the light is to not allow the darkness and demonic forces that surround us to overwhelm us. It is easy to become a slave to the news cycles these days. I confess that I wake up every morning and look to see what stupid tweets the president has posted during the night. I find myself increasingly overwhelmed by the threats to the well-being of the most vulnerable among us. We live in dangerous times where the rights of our neighbors and the health of the earth are constantly threatened. From Standing Rock to Charlottesville to Houston to Eagle Creek to Puerto Rico, the earth and our lives together are under attack.

However, long ago in a city called Ephesus, a small group of Christians could have easily been overwhelmed by the obstacles that they faced. Ephesus was a major port and center of trade in the ancient world. It was renowned as a center of learning with a leading library and for some a place of great prosperity where the wealthy elite lived in opulent homes. Religious pluralism flourished in Ephesus but with special attention given to the Temple of Artemis, one of the seven wonders of the world, dedicated to the goddess of fertility. In this urban setting, where the wealthy elite ruled the city, Christian faith was perceived as a threat. If you think that I am exaggerating, then simply go home and read Acts 19. For over two years, the Apostle Paul taught in Ephesus and led the early Christian community through experiences of miracles, healings, and growth. This fledgling group of Christians was perceived as a threat to commerce, religion, and the idolatry of its day because they dared to challenge the status quo of the day. Friends, the gospel of Jesus was and is a threat to the way of life in the empire. The conflict in Ephesus was so great that it is listed as a heading in my Bible: the riot in Ephesus—where Paul and other Christian leaders were chased out of the city.

It is in this context that these ancient words of encouragement come to us today: Live as children of the light. These words come not as some naïve, Pollyanna advice, but as a down-to-earth, incarnational way of living in difficult, threatening, and challenging times: Live as children of the light. Cultivate within yourself that which allows light to stay at the center of your life. Allow the light of Christ to shine in your life so that it will challenge the practices of greed and consumption that threaten our planet. Live in the light so that the darkness that surrounds us slowly recedes.

There's a second, equally revolutionary image in this text, for us to take with us. Ephesians 5 begins with these shocking words: "Be imitators of God." Be like God? Not something we hear very often in most of our congregations today. But in the early centuries of the church, many Christians found this image to be inspirational. For example, listen to the words of this letter from the second century:

> By loving God, you will be an imitator of God's goodness.
> Don't be surprised that a human can be an imitator of God.
> You can, if God wills it.
> For happiness consists not in lordship over one's neighbors,
> nor in possessing wealth and using force . . . .
> Whoever takes upon themselves the burden of their neighbor,
> Whoever desires to benefit one that is worse off . . .
> Whoever supplies to those that are in want . . .
> becomes . . . an imitator of God.[1]

Let me add to this list: whoever cares for the earth, whoever works for the restoration of our wetlands and waterways, whoever nurtures the land around us back to life becomes an imitator of God. For the One who created

---

1. Edited version of the *Letter to Diognetus* 10:4–6. Adapted from Ferguson, *Inherited Wisdom*, 172.

the earth and continues to breathe life and sustain us is the one who models for us the way to live into the future.

The surprising part of all of this is that it doesn't require superhuman effort on our part to imitate God. Becoming an imitator of God isn't about inflating our own sense of worth or trying to solve the problems of the universe on our own. Instead, it is about nurturing a steady determination to face the troubles that surround us and to remain diligent in our commitment to work for a better world. As light in the darkness, as those who work for the healing of the earth, as those who join with the Spirit in breathing life and hope into the places of pain in our own lives and into the world around us, we become imitators of the One who brings new life among us.

This morning, we conclude our time together by gathering around this table. Here on this table we gather around the gifts of this good earth— of bread and wine, like our brothers and sisters in the early church. As we share this meal together, the Spirit strengthens us for the journey ahead.

How will we live in the shadow of the empire that demands our allegiance? This morning, the words of Scripture offer us a way forward:

Live as children of the light. Be imitators of God. May these words from long ago guide us on our paths as we go from this place to work for the healing of the earth. To God be the glory. Amen.

Bibliography

Bannerman, D. D. *The Scottish Collects from the Scottish Metrical Psalter of 1595*. Occasional Paper, Church of Scotland. Edited by Patrick Millar. Committee on Public Worship and Aids to Devotion 5. Edinburgh: Church of Scotland Committee on Publications, 1933.

Barkley, John M. *Worship of the Reformed Church*. Richmond, VA: John Knox, 1967.

Barth, Karl. "Letter 207." April 4, 1966. https://postbarthian.com/2014/06/20/yes-us-karl-barths-final-words-emil-brunner/.

Benedict, Philip. *Christ's Churches Purely Reformed: A Social History of Calvinism*. New Haven: Yale University Press, 2002.

Berry, Thomas. *The Great Work: Our Way into the Future*. New York: Bell Tower, 1999.

Bieler, Andrea, and Luise Schottroff. *The Eucharist: Bodies, Bread, & Resurrection*. Minneapolis: Fortress, 2007.

Bonhoeffer, Dietrich. *Discipleship*. Edited by Geffrey B. Kelly and John D. Godsey. Translated by Barbara Green and Reinhard Krauss. Dietrich Bonhoeffer Works 4. Minneapolis: Fortress, 2003.

————. *Ethics*. Edited by Eberhard Bethge. Translated by Neville Horton Smith. Library of Philosophy and Theology. London: SCM, 1955.

The Book of Common Worship for the Presbyterian Church in the Republic of Korea. Seoul: PCRK, 2003.

Book of Divine Services, Vol. 1, The Services on Sundays, Holy Days, and Special Days. Karlsruhe: Verlags Druckerei Gebr. Tron KG, 1984.

Bowering, George. "Cascadia." In *Cascadia: The Elusive Utopia: Exploring the Spirit of the Pacific Northwest*, edited by Douglas Todd, 265–66. Vancouver: Ronsdale, 2008.

Bradshaw, Paul F. "Easter in Christian Tradition." In *Passover and Easter: Origin and History to Modern Times*, edited by Paul F. Bradshaw and Lawrence A. Hoffman, 1–7. Two Liturgical Traditions 5. Notre Dame, IN: University of Notre Dame Press, 1999.

————. *Eucharistic Origins*. Oxford: Oxford University Press, 2004.

Brown, Raymond E. *The Gospel According to John*. 2 vols. AB 29. Garden City, NY: Doubleday, 1966.

Bukowski, Peter. *Reformierte Liturgie: Gebete und Ordnungen für die unter dem Wort versammelte Gemeinde*. Wuppertal: Neukirchener Theologie, 1999.

Byars, Ronald P. *Lift Your Hearts on High: Eucharistic Prayer in the Reformed Tradition*. Louisville, KY: Westminster John Knox, 2005.

Calvin, Jean. *Calvin: Institutes of the Christian Religion*. Edited by John T. McNeill. Translated by Ford Lewis Battles. Philadelphia: Westminster, 1960.

Bibliography

————. *John Calvin: Writings on Pastoral Piety*. Edited by Elsie Anne McKee. Classics of Western Spirituality. New York: Paulist, 2001.

Campbell, Charles L. *Preaching Jesus: New Directions for Homiletics in Hans Frei's Postliberal Theology*. Grand Rapids: Eerdmans, 1997.

Carvalhaes, Cláudio. "'Gimme de Kneebone Bent': Liturgics, Dance, Resistance and a Hermeneutics of the Knees." *Studies in World Christianity* 14 (2008) 1–18.

Carvalhaes, Cláudio, and Paul Galbreath. "The Season of Easter: Imaginative Figurines for the Body of Christ." *Interpretation* 65 (2011) 5–16.

Chauvet, Louis-Marie. *Symbol and Sacrament: A Sacramental Reinterpretation of Christian Existence*. Translated by Patrick Madigan and Madeleine Beaumont. Collegeville, MN: Liturgical, 1995.

Chupungco, Anscar J. *Shaping the Easter Feast*. NPM Studies in Church Music and Liturgy. Washington, DC: Pastoral Press, 1992.

Churches Together in England. "Guidelines for Methods of Administration of Holy Communion and the Disposal of Remaining Eucharistic Elements." n.d. https://www.cte.org.uk/Publisher/File.aspx?id=10840.

Collaborative Ministry Office at Creighton University. "Remembering Archbishop Oscar Romero." Remembering the Assassination of Archbishop Oscar Romero. March 24, 1980, n.d. http://onlineministries.creighton.edu/CollaborativeMinistry/romero.html.

Connell, Martin. "From Easter to Pentecost." In *Passover and Easter: Origin and History to Modern Times*, edited by Paul F. Bradshaw and Lawrence A. Hoffman, 94–106. Two Liturgical Traditions 5. Notre Dame, IN: University of Notre Dame Press, 1999.

Daniels, Harold M. *To God Alone Be Glory: The Story and Sources of the Book of Common Worship*. Louisville, KY: Geneva, 2003.

Davies, J. G. *Holy Week: A Short History*. Ecumenical Studies in Worship 11. London: Lutterworth, 1963.

The Directory for the Publick Worship of God, Agreed Upon by the Assembly of Divines at Westminster, with the Assistance of Commissioners From the Church of Scotland. Philadelphia: Printed by Benjamin Franklin, 1745.

Diocese of Florida. "Diocesan Protocol for Use and Disposition of Consecrated Elements and Reserved Sacrament." March 17, 2010. http://dioceseofflorida.com/assets/use-of-consecrated-elements-and-reserved-sacrament.pdf.

Dorr, Kim. "Karl Barth: His 'No' to Natural Theology." http://www.belairpres.org/Content/Documents/Grow/Barth_his_no_to_natural_theology.pdf.

Dostoyevsky, Fyodor. *The Brothers Karamazov*. New York: Vintage, 1950.

Dyrness, William A. *Reformed Theology and Visual Culture: The Protestant Imagination from Calvin to Edwards*. Cambridge: Cambridge University Press, 2004.

Ferguson, Everett. *Inheriting Wisdom: Readings for Today from Ancient Christian Writers*. Peabody, MA: Hendrickson, 2004.

Fiddes, Paul S. *Past Event and Present Salvation: The Christian Idea of Atonement*. Louisville, KY: Westminster John Knox, 1989.

Frei, Hans W. *The Eclipse of Biblical Narrative: A Study in Eighteenth and Nineteenth Century Hermeneutics*. New Haven: Yale University Press, 1974.

————. "Theology and the Interpretation of Narrative: Some Hermeneutical Considerations." In *Theology and Narrative: Selected Essays*, edited by George Hunsinger and William C. Placher, 94–116. Oxford: Oxford University Press, 1993.

Galbreath, Paul. "Ash Wednesday: A Three Act Play in Turning, Nurturing, and Growing." Liturgy for Union Prebyterian Seminary Chapel, 2010.

———. "Doing Justice with a Sacramental Heart." *Hungryhearts* 14 (2005) 3–10.

———. *Doxology and Theology: An Investigation of the Apostles' Creed in Light of Ludwig Wittgenstein*. New York: P. Lang, 2008.

———. *Leading from the Table*. Herndon, VA: Alban Institute, 2008.

———. *Leading into the World*. Lanham, MD: Rowman & Littlefield, 2014.

———. "Sacramental Ethics: Making Public Worship Public." *Call to Worship: Liturgy, Music, Preaching & the Arts* 40 (2006) 56–61.

Gerlach, Karl. *The Antenicene Pascha: A Rhetorical History*. Liturgia Condenda 7. Leuven: Peeters, 1998.

Gerrish, B. A. "The Place of Calvin in Christian Theology." In *The Cambridge Companion to John Calvin*, edited by Donald K. McKim, 289–304. Cambridge, UK: Cambridge University Press, 2004.

Gibler, Linda. *From the Beginning to Baptism: Scientific and Sacred Stories of Water, Oil, and Fire*. Collegeville, MN: Liturgical, 2010.

Grow, Bobby. "No Theology Proper Behind the Back of Karl Barth: Just Say Nein to Theologies That Try to Talk God without the Primacy of Christ." *The Evangelical Calvinist*, August 3, 2017. https://growrag.wordpress.com/2017/08/03/no-theology-proper-behind-the-back-of-karl-barth-just-say-nein-to-theologies-that-try-to-talk-god-without-the-primacy-of-christ/.

Hair, Jesse. "Covenant and Care—a Baptismal Promise to Safeguard Creation." The Anglican Church of Canada, September 6, 2013. http://www.anglican.ca/news/covenant-and-care-a-baptismal-promise-to-safeguard-creation/3006799/.

Hall, Stanely R. "Becoming Christian: Ash Wednesday and the Sign of Ashes." *Reformed Liturgy & Music* 32 (1998) 191–95.

Hart, John. *Sacramental Commons: Christian Ecological Ethics*. Lanham, MD: Rowman & Littlefield, 2006.

Hessel, Dieter T. "The Church Ecologically Reformed." In *Earth Habitat: Eco-Injustice and the Church's Response*, edited by Larry L. Rasmussen and Dieter T. Hessel, 185–206. Minneapolis: Fortress, 2001.

Hoffman, Lawrence A. "The Passover Meal in Jewish Tradition." In *Passover and Easter: Origin and History to Modern Times*, edited by Paul F. Bradshaw and Lawrence A. Hoffman, 8–26. Two Liturgical Traditions 5. Notre Dame, IN: University of Notre Dame Press, 1999.

Horton, Michael. *Calvin on the Christian Life: Glorifying and Enjoying God Forever*. Wheaton, IL: Crossway, 2014.

Hurlbut, Stephen Augustus, ed. *The Liturgy of the Church of Scotland since the Reformation*. Washington, DC: St. Albans, 1944.

Immink, Gerrit. *The Touch of the Sacred: The Practice, Theology, and Tradition of Christian Worship*. Translated by Reinder Bruinsma. Grand Rapids: Eerdmans, 2014.

Johnson, Elizabeth A. *Ask the Beasts: Darwin and the God of Love*. London: Bloomsbury, 2014.

Jones, Serene. "Glorious Creation, Beautiful Law." In *Feminist and Womanist Essays in Reformed Dogmatics*, edited by Amy Plantinga Pauw and Serene Jones, 19–39. Columbia Series in Reformed Theology. Louisville, KY: Westminster John Knox, 2006.

Bibliography

Kermode, Frank. *The Genesis of Secrecy: On the Interpretation of Narrative*. Cambridge, MA: Harvard University Press, 1979.

Kierkegaard, Søren. *Concluding Unscientific Postscript to Philosophical Fragments*. Translated by David Swenson. Princeton: Princeton University Press, 1968.

Klinghardt, Matthias. "A Typology of the Communal Meal." In *Meals in the Early Christian World*, 9–22. New York: Palgrave Macmillan, 2012.

Knox, John. *The Liturgy of John Knox: Received by the Church of Scotland in 1564*. Glasgow: Glasgow University Press, 1886.

———. *The Liturgy of John Knox: Received by the Church of Scotland in 1564*. Eugene, OR: Wipf & Stock, 2009.

Lathrop, Gordon. *Holy People: A Liturgical Ecclesiology*. Minneapolis: Fortress, 2006.

Leishman, Thomas, ed. *The Westminster Directory: For the Publique Worship of God*. Edinburgh: Blackwood, 1901.

Liturgie de L'église Réformée de France. Lyon: Olivetan, 2010.

Long, Kimberly. "A New Worship Book for the Presbyterian Church (USA)." *PrayTellBlog*. http://www.praytellblog.com/index.php/2017/09/17/a-new-worship-book-for-the-presbyterian-church-usa/.

Lutheran World Federation. *Christian Worship: Unity in Cultural Diversity*. Edited by S. Anita Stauffer. LWF Studies. Geneva: Lutheran World Federation, 1996.

Lyotard, Jean-François. *The Postmodern Condition: A Report on Knowledge*. Translated by Geoff Bennington and Brian Massumi. Theory and History of Literature 10. Minneapolis: University of Minnesota Press, 1984.

Macalintal, Diana. "History of the Scrutinies: 3 Things Your RCIA Team Needs to Know." TeamRCIA, March 3, 2009. http://teamrcia.com/2009/03/a-brief-history-of-the-scrutinies-and-why-it-matters/.

McGowan, Andrew Brian. "The Myth of the 'Lord's Supper': Paul's Eucharistic Meal Terminology and Its Ancient Reception." *Catholic Biblical Quarterly* 77 (2015) 503–21.

McGrath, Alister E. *Emil Brunner: A Reappraisal*. Chichester: Wiley Blackwell, 2014.

Metz, Johann Baptist. *Faith in History and Society: Toward a Practical Fundamental Theology*. Translated by David Smith. New York: Seabury, 1980.

Moore, Gerard. "The Vocabulary of the Collects: Retrieving a Biblical Heritage." In *Appreciating the Collect: An Irenic Methodology*, edited by James G. Leachman and Daniel P. McCarthy, 175–95. Farnborough: St. Michael's Abbey, 2008.

O'Loughlin, Thomas. *The Eucharist: Origins and Contemporary Understandings*. London: Bloomsbury Academic, 2015.

Pauw, Amy Plantinga. "The Graced Infirmity of the Church." In *Feminist and Womanist Essays in Reformed Dogmatics*, edited by Amy Plantinga Pauw and Serene Jones, 189–203. Columbia Series in Reformed Theology. Louisville, KY: Westminster John Knox, 2006.

Pendergrast, Mark. *Mirror Mirror: A History of the Human Love Affair with Reflection*. New York: Basic Books, 2003.

Power, David N. *Sacrament: The Language of God's Giving*. New York: Crossroad, 1999.

Presbyterian Church (U.S.A.). *Book of Common Worship*. Louisville, KY: Westminster John Knox, 1993.

———. *The Book of Common Worship*. Philadelphia: Board of Christian Education of the Presbyterian Church in the USA, 1946.

———. *Book of Occasional Services*. Louisville, KY: Geneva, 1999.

———. "Commissioning to Ministry Outside a Congregation." In *Book of Occasional Services*, 129–34. Louisville, KY: Geneva, 1999.

———. *The Constitution of the Presbyterian Church (U.S.A.): Part I, Book of Confessions.* Offices of the General Assembly, 1988.

———. *The Constitution of the Presbyterian Church (U.S.A.): Part II, Book of Order.* Louisville, KY: Offices of the General Assembly, 1988.

———. *The Service for the Lord's Day: The Worship of God.* Supplemental Liturgical Resource 1. Philadelphia: Westminster, 1984.

———. *Service for the Lord's Day and Lectionary for the Christian Year.* Philadelphia: Westminster, 1964.

———. *The Worshipbook: Services.* Philadelphia: Westminister, 1970.

Rasmussen, Larry L. *Earth-Honoring Faith: Religious Ethics in a New Key.* New York: Oxford University Press, 2013.

———. "Eco-Justice: Church and Community Together." In *Earth Habitat: Eco-Injustice and the Church's Response*, edited by Larry L. Rasmussen and Dieter T. Hessel, 1–22. Minneapolis, MN: Fortress, 2001.

Research Services, Presbyterian Church (U.S.A.). "The Sacraments: The Report of the February 2009 Presbyterian Panel Survey." Louisville, KY, 2011. https://www.presbyterianmission.org/wp-content/uploads/panel13-feb2009s.pdf.

Regan, Patrick. "The Collect in Context." In *Appreciating the Collect: An Irenic Methodology*, edited by James G. Leachman and Daniel P. McCarthy, 83–99. Farnborough: St. Michael's Abbey, 2008.

Ricœur, Paul. *The Philosophy of Paul Ricœur: An Anthology of His Work.* Edited by Charles E. Reagan and David Stewart. Boston: Beacon, 1978.

Rite of Christian Initiation of Adults. Collegeville, MN: Liturgical Press, 1998.

Ross, Susan A. *Extravagant Affections: A Feminist Sacramental Theology.* New York: Continuum, 1998.

Santmire, H. Paul. *Ritualizing Nature: Renewing Christian Liturgy in a Time of Crisis.* Minneapolis: Fortress, 2008.

Satterlee, Craig Alan. *Ambrose of Milan's Method of Mystagogical Preaching.* Collegeville, MN: Liturgical, 2002.

Smith, Dennis E. *From Symposium to Eucharist: The Banquet in the Early Christian World.* Minneapolis: Fortress, 2003.

———. "The Greco-Roman Banquet as a Social Institution." In *Meals in the Early Christian World*, edited by Dennis E. Smith and Hal Taussig, 23–33. New York: Palgrave Macmillan, 2012.

Smith, Dennis E., and Hal Taussig. *Many Tables: The Eucharist in the New Testament and Liturgy Today.* Philadelphia: Trinity International, 1990.

———, eds. *Meals in the Early Christian World: Social Formation, Experimentation, and Conflict at the Table.* New York: Palgrave Macmillan, 2012.

Spinks, Bryan D. *Early and Medieval Rituals and Theologies of Baptism: From the New Testament to the Council of Trent.* Aldershot, UK: Ashgate, 2006.

Stevenson, Kenneth. *Jerusalem Revisited.* Washington, DC: Pastoral Press, 1988.

Strathdee, Jim & Jean. "Holy Is the Night." Track 15 on *Miracle of Dawn*, music recording. Jim & Jean Strathdee, 2017.

Taft, Robert F. "Mass Without the Consecration? The Historic Agreement on the Eucharist Between the Catholic Church and the Assyrian Church of the East Promulgated 26 October 2001." *Worship* 77 (2003) 482–509.

Bibliography

Taussig, Hal. *In the Beginning Was the Meal: Social Experimentation and Early Christian Identity*. Minneapolis: Fortress, 2009.

Taylor, Charles. *A Secular Age*. Cambridge, MA: Belknap, 2007.

Thompson, Bard. *Liturgies of the Western Church*. New York: Meridian, 1961.

United Presbyterian Church in the U.S.A. *The Calvin Strasbourg Service: A Re-Enactment in Dramatic Terms of an Authentic 16th Century Worship Service Based on John Calvin's Strasbourg Liturgy*. Philadelphia: Board of Christian Education, 1959.

Veloso, Caetano. *O Quereres*. Personalidade. Polygram, 1993.

White, James F. *Introduction to Christian Worship*. Nashville: Abingdon, 2000.

Wilkinson, John, ed. *Egeria's Travels to the Holy Land*. Jerusalem: Ariel, 1981.

Wittgenstein, Ludwig. *Culture and Value*. Edited by G. H. von Wright. Translated by Peter Winch. Oxford: Blackwell, 1980.

———. *Philosophical Investigations*. Translated by G. E. M. Anscombe. Oxford: Blackwell, 1953.

———. *Zettel*. Edited by G. E. M. Anscombe and G. H. von Wright. Translated by G. E. M. Anscombe. Berkeley: University of California Press, 1970.

World Council of Churches, ed. *Baptism, Eucharist and Ministry*. Toronto: Anglican Book Centre, 1983.

"Yes to Us All: Karl Barth's Final Words to Emil Brunner." *The PostBarthian,* June 20, 2014. https://postbarthian.com/2014/06/20/yes-us-karl-barths-final-words-emil-brunner/.

Zachman, Randall C. *Reconsidering John Calvin*. Current Issues in Theology. Cambridge, UK: Cambridge University Press, 2012.